ISBN 978-1-332-73369-9
PIBN 10290747

1 MONTH OF
FREE
READING

at
www.ForgottenBooks.com

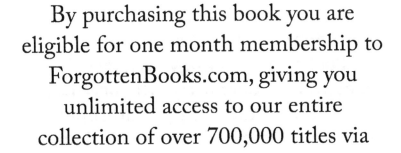

By purchasing this book you are eligible for one month membership to ForgottenBooks.com, giving you unlimited access to our entire collection of over 700,000 titles via our web site and mobile apps.

To claim your free month visit:
www.forgottenbooks.com/free290747

English
Français
Deutsche
Italiano
Español
Português

www.forgottenbooks.com

Mythology Photography **Fiction**
Fishing Christianity **Art** Cooking
Essays Buddhism Freemasonry
Medicine **Biology** Music **Ancient
Egypt** Evolution Carpentry Physics
Dance Geology **Mathematics** Fitness
Shakespeare **Folklore** Yoga Marketing
Confidence Immortality Biographies
Poetry **Psychology** Witchcraft
Electronics Chemistry History **Law**
Accounting **Philosophy** Anthropology
Alchemy Drama Quantum Mechanics
Atheism Sexual Health **Ancient History**
Entrepreneurship Languages Sport
Paleontology Needlework Islam
Metaphysics Investment Archaeology
Parenting Statistics Criminology
Motivational

INTRODUCTION TO ACTUARIAL SCIENCE

By

HARRY ANSON FINNEY

AMERICAN INSTITUTE OF ACCOUNTANTS

NEW YORK

Copyright, 1920,
By HARRY ANSON FINNEY

INTRODUCTORY NOTE

Part of the text of *Introduction to Actuarial Science* appeared originally in *The Journal of Accountancy* for November and December, 1919.

The copyright was donated by the author to the endowment fund of the American Institute of Accountants, and, in response to suggestions, the author added solutions of actuarial problems which had appeared in the examinations of the Institute.

The text is published in book form under the endowment fund of the Institute.

There has long been a demand for a clear, elementary text on actuarial science, and it is hoped that the demand will be fully met by this volume.

The American Institute of Accountants is under a debt of gratitude to Mr. Finney for preparing the matter contained in this book and for his generous donation of the copyright to the endowment fund.

A. P. RICHARDSON,
Secretary.

New York, June, 1920.

TABLE OF CONTENTS

INTRODUCTION TO ACTUARIAL
SCIENCE

Introduction to Actuarial Science

In the more comprehensive meaning of the term, actuarial science includes an expert knowledge of the principles of compound interest as well as the laws of insurance probabilities. Public accountants, however, are usually interested only in the interest phases of actuarial science, leaving the application of the laws of insurance probabilities to the actuary, who ascertains the measurement of risks and establishes tables of rates. This discussion of actuarial science will, therefore, be restricted to the phases thereof which deal with compound interest.

There seems to be a more or less prevalent belief that the exacting of compound interest is illegal, and that this illegality makes the mathematics of compound interest an impractical matter of purely academic importance. While it may be illegal in some jurisdictions for a creditor to charge the debtor interest on unpaid interest, there can be no legal restriction against the collection and reinvestment of the interest. In fact, the mathematical theory of investment is based on the assumption that all interest accretions become themselves a part of the investment, being converted at periodical intervals into interest-earning principal. The compound interest basis is the only scientific one where the accumulation or reduction of an investment extends over a series of periods. It is with compound interest, therefore, and not with simple interest, that actuarial science deals.

Interest is the increase in investment or indebtedness caused by the use of money or credit. The rapidity and extent of the increase depend on the factors of interest, which are rate, frequency and time.

The rate is usually expressed in terms of percentage and measures the fraction by which the investment is increased at each date of conversion of interest. Thus, a rate of 5% per period indicates that the interest each period will be .05 of the investment at the beginning of the period; or, stated in another way, the investment at the end of the period will be 1.05 times the investment at the beginning of the period. Expressing the decimal interest rate by the symbol i (for instance, .05 $= i$), the interest earned during any period may be computed by multiplying the investment at the beginning of the period by i; and the increased investment at the end of each period may be computed by multiplying the investment at the beginning of the period by

1+i. The symbol 1+i is called the ratio of increase, because it measures the ratio existing between the investment at the beginning and the investment at the end of each period.

The frequency is the length of the period in years, months or days between the dates of interest conversions. It is evident that the frequency of compounding will materially affect the rapidity with which an investment increases. For instance, an investment of $1.00 for one year will amount to more if the loan is at 1½% per period of 3 months than if at 6% per period of 12 months.

Increase during one year in investment of $1.00 at 1½% per period of 3 months:

```
                1.00  — · original investment
   Multiply by  1.015    ratio of increase
                ─────
                1.015     investment end of 3 months
    "       "   1.015
                ────────
                1.030225   "        "   " 6    "
    "       "   1.015
                ────────
                1.045678   ··       "   " 9    "
    "       "   1.015
                ────────
                1.061364   "        "   " 12   "
```

Increase during one year in investment of $1.00 at 6% per period of 12 months:

```
                1.00   original investment
   Multiply by  1.06   ratio of increase
                ─────
                1.06   investment end of 12 months
```

One frequently sees interest tables in which the interest rates are stated as a certain per cent. per annum. It is better to express the rate as a certain per cent. per period, because, when the compounding occurs more frequently than once a year, the effective rate earned during a year is really greater than the nominal rate. Thus, in the foregoing illustration, the loan is made at $1\frac{1}{2}\%$ per period of three months. The customary statement, however, is that the rate is 6% a year compounded quarterly. The nominal rate is 6%, but since the investment increases during the year from 1.00 to 1.061364, the effective rate per annum is 6.1364%.

The time is the total number of periods over which the investment extends. It is customary in commercial parlance to state the time as a certain number of years, but as a matter of principle the time is a certain number of periods which may be of any duration, and the rate should, therefore, be stated as the rate per period. For instance, if money is lent at 6% per annum for $4\frac{1}{2}$ years, compounded semi-annually, the time (represented by the symbol n) is 9 periods, and the rate (represented by i) is 3% per period.

Each dollar of an investment increases in the same ratio as every other dollar; therefore, in compound interest computations, it is customary to compute the required value on the basis of a principal of $1.00, and to multiply by the number of dollars in the principal.

THE AMOUNT OF 1.

Since interest increases the investment, the fundamental problem in interest is the computation of the amount to which an investment will increase in a given time. It has already been noted that the increase depends upon i (the rate per period) and n (the number of periods). During each period the investment increases in the ratio of $1+i$. At 6% per period, an investment of 1 will amount, at the end of 1 period, to 1.06, or $1+i$; during the next period the investment will increase to 1.06, the investment at the beginning of the period, multiplied by 1.06, the ratio of increase, or to 1.1236, which is $(1+i)^2$; at the end of the third period the investment will amount to 1.1236, the investment at the beginning of the period, multiplied by 1.06, or 1.191016, which is $(1+i)^3$. Or, stated generally, the investment will amount at the end of n periods to $(1+i)^n$.

This means that the ratio of increase is raised to the nth power, or that the amount is a product obtained by using the ratio of increase as a factor as many times as there are periods. Representing the amount of 1 by S, the formula is

$$S = (1+i)^n$$

When compound interest tables are available, the amount can be determined by reference to them. A table of amounts appears as follows:

AMOUNT OF 1 AT COMPOUND INTEREST

Periods	3%	3½%	4%	4½%	5%
1	1.030000	1.035000	1.040000	1.045000	1.050000
2	1.060900	1.071225	1.081600	1.092025	1.102500
3	1.092727	1.108718	1.124864	1.141166	1.157625
4	1.125509	1.147523	1.169859	1.192519	1.215506
5	1.159274	1.187686	1.216653	1.246182	1.276282
6	1.194052	1.229255	1.265319	1.302260	1.340096
7	1.229874	1.272279	1.315932	1.360862	1.407100
8	1.266770	1.316809	1.368569	1.422101	1.477455

When interest tables are not available, the amount is easily computed by logarithms. To illustrate: what is the amount of 1 at 6% compound interest for 4 years, compounded semi-annually?

$S = 1.03^8$

The logarithm of 1.03 is   .012837
To raise to the 8th power multiply by   8
                                                          ─────────
The product is   .102696, which is
the logarithm of 1.266764, or 1.03^8.
An interest table states this amount as 1.266770

When neither an interest table nor a table of logarithms is available, the amount may be computed by repeated multiplications. The required amount is the product obtained by using the ratio of increase as a factor as many times as there are periods. Thus, 1.03^8 may be computed as follows:

1.03
1.03
——
1.0609 amount at end of 2 periods
1.03
——
1.092727 ··   ··   ^   ··
1.03
——
1.125509 ··   ··   4   ··
1.03
——
1.159274 "   "   5   "
1.03
——
1.194052 "   "   6   "
1.03
——
1.229874 ··   ··   7   ··
1.03
——
1.266770 "   "   8   "

This work can be materially reduced by recognizing the principle that the multiplication of any two powers of a number results in a power represented by an exponent equal to the sum of the exponents of the powers multiplied. For instance, $1.0609 = 1.03^2$.

Now since 1.0609 contains 1.03 twice as a factor, the product of 1.0609 multiplied by 1.0609 will contain 1.03 four times as a factor. Thus

$$1.0609 \times 1.0609 = 1.125509 = 1.03^4$$

The eighth power can be obtained thus:

        1.125509   the 4th power
multiplied by 1.125509   " 4   "
        ——————
        1.266770   " 8   ··

The seventh power can be obtained by multiplying any powers the sum of whose exponents is 7.

Thus:		Or:	
1.092727	the 3rd power	1.0609	the 2nd power
1.125509	" 4th "	1.159274	" 5th "
1.229874	" 7th "	1.229874	" 7th "

This principle may be applied when it is desired to determine an amount beyond the scope of an interest table. Thus, if an interest table extends only to 20 periods, the amount for, say, 75 periods, can be computed by multiplication of the amounts for periods within the scope of the table, as follows:

$$20\text{th} \times 20\text{th} \times 20\text{th} \times 15\text{th} = 75\text{th}$$

Or the principle may be applied when an amount must be computed with no table available. For instance, $(1+i)^{35}$ may be computed thus:

$$(1+i) \times (1+i) = (1+i)^2$$
$$(1+i)^2 \times (1+i)^2 = (1+i)^4$$
$$(1+i)^4 \times (1+i)^4 = (1+i)^8$$
$$(1+i)^8 \times (1+i)^8 = (1+i)^{16}$$
$$(1+i)^{16} \times (1+i)^{16} = (1+i)^{32}$$
$$(1+i)^{32} \times (1+i)^2 = (1+i)^{34}$$
$$(1+i)^{34} \times (1+i) = (1+i)^{35}$$

THE COMPOUND INTEREST

Since the interest increases the investment, the difference between 1 and the amount of 1 is the compound interest. Representing the compound interest by the symbol I,

$$I = S - 1$$

Illustration: required the compound interest on 1 at 6% per annum for 4 years, compounded semi-annually?

The amount of 1.03^8 has already been computed as 1.266770.

Then $1.266770 - 1 = .266770$ the compound interest.

THE RATE

When the investment, the amount and the time are known, the rate can be computed by logarithms.

Illustration: if $80.00 invested at an unknown rate, compounded annually will amount to $107.20 in six years, what is the rate?

$$80 \times (1+i)^6 = 107.20$$

thats → Way Hence $(1+i)^6 = 107.20 \div 80 = 1.34$; $(1+i)^6 = \sqrt[6]{1.34}$

Since 1.34 is the 6th power of $1+i$, it is necessary to extract the 6th root, which is accomplished as follows:

log. $1.34 = .127105$
log. $\sqrt[6]{1.34} = .127105 \div 6 = .021184$

.021184 is almost the exact logarithm of 1.05, or $1+i$

Hence $i = .05$ the rate.

THE TIME

When the investment, amount and rate are known, the time can be computed by logarithms.

Illustration: for how many years must $2,-
000.00 remain at 5% interest compounded annually to produce $5,054.00?

Since $$5054 = 2000 \times 1.05^n$$
$$5054 \div 2000 = 1.05^n$$
$$\text{Or } 2.527 = 1.05^n$$
$$\log. \ 2.527 = .402605$$
$$\log. \ 1.05 = .021189$$
$$.402605 \div .021189 = 19, \text{ the number of years.}$$

PRESENT VALUE OF I

The present value of a sum due at a fixed
future date is a smaller sum which, with interest,
will amount to the future sum.   When the time
is more than one period, the smaller sum will
accumulate at compound interest, increasing each
period in the ratio of increase of $1+i$.

Representing the present value by the symbol P
the accumulated sum at the end of 1 period will be $P \times (1+i)$
"   "   " "   "   " " 2 periods " " $P \times (1+i)^2$
"   "   " "   "   " "n   "   " " $P \times (1+i)^n$

Where the future sum is 1
$$P \times (1+i)^n = 1$$
and since
$$(1+i)^n = S$$
$$P \times S = 1$$
or
$$P = 1 \div S$$

That is, the present value of 1 due n periods
hence at a given rate may be computed by dividing 1 by the amount of 1 for n periods at the same
rate.

Illustration: what is the present value of 1. due four periods hence at 3%?

The table of amounts of 1 at 3% shows that $1.03^4 = 1.125509$.

Then $1 \div 1.125509 = .888487$, which is the present value of 1 at 3% for 4 periods as shown in the following illustrative table:

PRESENT VALUE OF 1

Periods	3%	3½%	4%	4½%	5%
1	.970874	.966184	.961538	.956938	.952381
2	.942596	.933511	.924556	.915730	.907029
3	.915142	.901943	.888996	.876297	.863838
4	.888487	.871442	.854804	.838561	.822702
5	.862609	.841973	.821927	.802451	.783526
6	.837484	.813501	.790315	.767896	.746215
7	.813092	.785991	.759918	.734828	.710681
8	.789409	.759412	.730690	.703185	.676839

When a table of present values is not available the value of P can be computed by dividing 1 by the value of S for the same time and rate, shown by a table of amounts of 1.

In the absence of any table, the value of P can be computed in one of the following ways:

Required: the present value of 1 due 4 periods hence at 3%.

Compute the value of S, which in this case is 1.03^4, and divide 1 by the value of S.

$$1.03^2 = 1.0609$$
$$1.03^4 = 1.0609^2 = 1.125509$$
$$1 \div 1.125509 = .888487$$

Or, use the ratio of increase as a divisor as many times as there are periods, using 1 as the first dividend, and each quotient as the dividend in the succeeding division; thus:

$$1 \div 1.03 = .970874 \text{ present value of 1 due 1 period hence}$$
$$.970874 \div 1.03 = .942596 \text{ " " " 1 " 2 periods "}$$
$$.942596 \div 1.03 = .915142 \text{ " " " 1 " 3 " "}$$
$$.915142 \div 1.03 = .888487 \text{ " " " 1 " 4 " "}$$

Or, divide 1 by the ratio of increase, and raise the quotient to the nth power; thus:

$$1 \div 1.03 = .970874$$
$$.970874 \times .970874 = .942596 \text{ present value of 1 due 2 periods hence}$$
$$.942596 \times .942596 = .888487 \text{ " " " 1 " 4 " "}$$

Compound Discount

The present value of 1 is the sum which will accumulate to 1 in a given time at a given rate. The difference between 1 and the present value of 1 is the compound discount, which will be represented by the symbol D. The compound discount can be computed by the formula:

$$D = 1 - P$$

Illustration: required the compound discount on 1 due 4 periods hence at 3%.

The value of P for 4 periods at 3% was computed above. It is .888487.

Therefore $1 - .888487 = .111513$, the compound discount.

This is the formula to use when one has a table of present values. If one has only a table of amounts of 1, it is better to use the formula:

$$D = I \div S$$

This formula requires explanation. The compound discount is really the compound interest earned on the present value. It is the interest which increases P to 1. For instance, if one lends .888487 for 4 periods at 3%, the interest will be .111513, increasing the investment to 1.

Now the interest earned is proportionate to the sum invested. If the investment is 1, the compound interest will be I. If the investment is half of 1, the compound interest will be ½ of I. If the investment is .888487, the interest will be I x .888487. That is, if the investment is P the earning of D will be I x P. But P is 1 ÷ S.

Hence the formula:

$$D = I \times P$$

may be stated $$D = I \times (1 \div S)$$

or $$D = I \times \frac{1}{S}$$

or $$D = I \div S$$

To illustrate the application of this formula: required the compound discount on 1 for 4 periods at 3%. Given: $1.03^4 = 1.125509$.

Then .125509 ÷ 1.125509 = .111513.

ANNUITIES

A series of equal payments, running supposedly for more than a year and due at regular intervals, is an annuity. The intervals may be periods of any length, as a month, a quarter, a half year or a year. The periodical payments of an annuity are usually called rents.

Since the rents may be invested when received, there is the problem of determining the amount to which the rents will accumulate. On the other hand it may be desired to compute the investment which, with interest accumulations, will permit the withdrawal of rents of stated amounts at stated intervals. The sum so invested is the present value of the annuity. These are the two fundamental annuity problems. The amount of an immediate annuity of 1 per period for n periods will be represented by the symbol s_n; the present value of an immediate annuity of 1 per period for n periods, by the sumbol a_n.

AMOUNT OF ANNUITY

To illustrate the methods of computing the amount to which the rents of an annuity will accumulate, let it be assumed that a contract requires the following payments:

Dec. 31, 1916	$300.00
" 31, 1917	300.00
" 31, 1918	300.00
" 31, 1919	300.00

Required the amount to which these payments will accumulate at December 31, 1919, if each rent is invested immediately at 3% per annum,

Clearly the amount of the annuity will be the sum of the four $300 rents plus the interest on each rent, as follows:

Date	Rent	Periods at interest	Amount of 1	Amount of 300
Dec. 31, 1916	$300.00	3	1.092727	327.8181
" 31, 1917	300.00	2	1.0609	318.27
" 31, 1918	300.00	1	1.03	309.00
" 31, 1919	300.00	0	1.00	300.00
	1200.00			1255.0881

Although the amount of an annuity may be computed by determining the amount of each rent and the sum of these amounts, it is unnecessary to resort to this labor.

The following short method may be used:

To find the amount of an annuity of 1 for a given number of periods at a given rate, divide the compound interest on 1 for the number of periods at the given rate by the simple interest rate. Or, in symbols:

$$s_{\overline{n}|} = I \div i$$

Applied to the foregoing illustration:

$$1.03^4 = 1.125509$$

Hence $I = .125509$

And $s_{\overline{4}|} = .125509 \div .03 = 4.18363$, the amount of an annuity of 1

$4.18363 \times 300 = 1255.089$, the amount of an annuity of 300

The accumulation of this annuity may be shown thus:

December 31, 1916	Rent	$300.00
" 31, 1917	Interest at 3% on $300.00	9.00
	Rent	300.00
	Total	$609.00
" 31, 1918	Interest at 3% on $609.00	18.27
	Rent	300.00
	Total	$927.27
" 31, 1919	Interest at 3% on $927.27	27.82
	Rent	300.00
	Total	$1,255.09

To understand the formula $s_{\overline{n}|} = I \div i$, it is necessary to consider the relation between compound interest and the amount of an annuity. To show this relation, we shall assume that the four $300.00 payments referred to in the preceding illustration represented the annual interest on $10,000.00 at 3%, the money being lent one year before the first interest payment was due. The four payments of $300.00 each, or $1,200.00 altogether, constitute the simple interest at 3% on $10,000.00 for four years. By investing each $300.00 payment at 3%, the creditor makes his investment pay compound interest, because he earns interest on the interest. The sum of $1,255.089 is, therefore, the compound interest at 3% for four periods on $10,000.00. It is also the amount of an annuity of four rents of $300.00 each, accumulating at 3%, as shown by the two foregoing solutions. Expressed formally as equations,

$1,255.089 = I on $10,000.00 (compound interest on $10,000.00).

and also

$1,255.089 = $s_{\overline{4}|}$ of $300.00 (amount of annuity of $300.)

Dividing $1,255.089 by 10,000,

$.1255089 = I on $1

$= s_{\overline{4}|}$ of $.03

Or, in other words, the compound interest on $1 at 3% for four periods is equal to the amount of an annuity of $.03 for four periods at 3%. Now, if .1255089 is the amount of an annuity of 3 cents for four periods at 3%, .1255089 ÷ 3 is the amount of an annuity of 1 cent for four periods at 3%; and .1255089 ÷ .03 is the amount of an annuity of $1 for four periods at 3%. Since .1255089 is also the compound interest on 1 for four periods at 3%, represented by I; and since .03 is the interest rate, represented by i,

$$I \div i = s_{\overline{n}|}$$

Interest books usually contain tables showing the amounts of annuities, in the following form:

AMOUNT OF ANNUITY OF I

Periods	3%	3½%	4%	4½%	5%
1	1.000000	1.000000	1.000000	1.000000	1.000000
2	2.030000	2.035000	2.040000	2.045000	2.050000
3	3.090900	3.106225	3.121600	3.137025	3.152500
4	4.183627	4.214943	4.246464	4.278191	4.310125
5	5.309136	5.362466	5.416323	5.470710	5.525631
6	6.468410	6.550152	6.632975	6.716892	6.801913
7	7.662462	7.779408	7.898294	8.019152	8.142008
8	8.892336	9.051687	9.214226	9.380014	9.549109

AMOUNT OF AN ANNUITY DUE

The above formula for determining the amount of an annuity applies only to an ordinary or immediate annuity. It must be modified slightly to be applicable to an annuity due.

An ordinary or immediate annuity is one whose rents are due at the ends of the periods. An annuity due is one whose rents are due at the beginnings of the periods. Since the last rent of an ordinary annuity is due at the end of the last period, no interest is earned after the payment of the last rent. But in the case of an annuity due, the last rent is paid in at the beginning of the last period, and hence all rents as well as the accumulated interest thereon bear interest for another period.

The difference between these two classes of annuities may be made more apparent by the following table comparing an ordinary annuity, the rents being payable at the end of each period, and an annuity due, the rents being payable at the beginning of each period.

Year	Ordinary annuity Rents due	Annuity due Rents due
1916		January 1
	December 31	
1917		January 1
	December 31	
1918		January 1
	December 31	
1919		January 1
	December 31	

It is evident that if the rents and the interest rates of the two annuities are the same, the amount of the four rents of the ordinary annuity, at December 31, 1919, will be the same as the amount of the four rents of the annuity due at January 1, 1919, because in each case there will be three interest accretions. But in the case of the annuity due, the entire amount accumulated at January 1, 1919, will earn interest for a full period to December 31, 1919, the end of the last period. This will cause an increase computed by multiplying by the ratio of increase, $1+i$. Representing the amount of an annuity due of 1 per period for n periods by the symbol $s_{\overline{n}|}$, the formula for the amount of an annuity due is:

$$s_{\overline{n}|} = (I \div i) \times (1+i)$$

This means that the amount of an annuity due may be computed by determining the amount of an ordinary annuity of the same rents for the same number of periods and at the same rate and multiplying this amount by the ratio of increase.

Illustration: if $300 is deposited on January 1, 1916, 1917, 1918 and 1919, at 3%, what will be the amount of the annuity one year after making the last deposit?

$s_{\overline{4}|} = (.125509 \div .03) \times 1.03$
    $= 4.18363 \times 1.03$
    $= 4.309139$, amount of annuity due of 1
$4.309139 \times 300 = 1,292.74$, amount of annuity due of 300.

This method is a convenient one to employ when the amount of an ordinary annuity has been computed and it is desired to compute the amount of an annuity due of the same number of rents at the same rate per period. The amount of an annuity due for n periods may also be computed by determining the amount of an ordinary annuity of $n+1$ periods and deducting one rent. Applying the method to the above illustration, the solution would be:

First, if a table of annuity amounts is available:

> The table shows the amount of an ordinary annuity of four rents of 1 at 3%, to be 5.309136.
>
> Then $5.309136-1=4.309136$, the amount of an annuity due of four rents.

Second, if a table of annuity amounts is not available:

> The amount of 1 at compound interest for five periods at 3% may be computed, or ascertained from a table. It is 1.159274.
>
> Then $.159274 \div .03 = 5.309133$, the amount of an ordinary annuity of 1 for five periods.
>
> And $5.309133 - 1 = 4.309133$, the amount of an annuity due of 1 for four periods.
>
> And $4.309133 \times 300 = 1,292.74$, the amount of an annuity due of 300 for four periods.

The accumulation of this annuity may be shown thus:

January 1, 1916	Rent	300.00
January 1, 1917	Interest at 3% on 300.00	9.00
	Rent	300.00
	Total	609.00
January 1, 1918	Interest at 3% on 609.00	18.27
	Rent	300.00
	Total	927.27
January 1, 1919	Interest at 3% on 927.27	27.82
	Rent	300.00
	Total	1,255.09
January 1, 1920	Interest at 3% on 1,255.09	37.65
	Total	1,292.74

SINKING FUND CONTRIBUTIONS

When the amount of each contribution to a sinking fund is computed on an actuarial basis, instead of on an arbitrary or a per-unit-of-output basis, the problem is to determine the periodical rents which will produce a required amount. The periodical contribution is computed by determining the amount of an annuity of $1 for the given number of periods at the given rate. The amount of the required fund is then divided by the amount of an annuity of $1. Since it is customary to deposit the periodical contributions at the ends of the periods, the divisor is usually the amount of an ordinary annuity. Representing the total fund by the symbol S.F. and the periodical contributions by S.F.C.,

$$S.F.C. = S.F. \div s_{\overline{n}|}$$

Illustration: a company borrowed $25,000.00 for four years, and provided for its repayment by establishing a sinking fund on a 3% basis, the contributions being made at the end of each of the four years. What was the amount of each contribution?

The amount of an ordinary annuity of 1 for four periods at 3% has already been computed at 4.18363.

Then

$$S.F.C. = 25,000 \div 4.18363$$
$$= 5,975.67$$

The following table shows the accumulation of the fund on a 3% basis:

SINKING FUND TABLE

End of 1st year:		
Contribution		5,975.67
End of 2nd year:		
Interest at 3% on 5,975.67:	179.27	
Contribution	5,975.67	6,154.94
Total		12,130.61
End of 3rd year:		
Interest at 3% on 12,130.61:	363.92	
Contribution	5,975.67	6,339.59
Total		18,470.20
End of 4th year:		
Interest at 3% on 18,470.20:	554.11	
Contribution	5,975.67	6,529.78
Total		24,999.98

Or the accumulation of the fund could be shown thus:

SINKING FUND TABLE

Year	Interest	Contribution	Total
1		5,975.67	5,975.67
2	179.27	5,975.67	12,130.61
3	363.92	5,975.67	18,470.20
4	554.11	5,975.67	24,999.98
Total	1,097.30	23,902.68	

If the contributions were made at the beginning of each period it would be necessary to divide the total fund by the amount of an annuity due.

Illustration: referring to the preceding illustration, what would be the amount of each contribution if the company made the deposits at the beginning of each year?

The amount of an annuity due of 1 for four periods at 3% has already been computed at 4.309139.

Then $S.F.C. = 25,000 \div 4.309139$
$$= 5,801.62$$

The accumulation of the sinking fund may be tabulated as follows:

SINKING FUND TABLE

First Year:

Beginning:	Contribution	5,801.62
End:	Interest on 5,801.62	174.05
		5,975.67

Second Year:

Beginning:	Contribution	5,801.62
		11,777.29
End:	Interest on 11,777.29	353.32
		12,130.61

Third Year

Beginning:	Contribution	5,801.62
		17,932.23
End:	Interest on 17,932.23	537.97
		18,470.20

Fourth Year:

Beginning:	Contribution	5,801.62
		24,271.82
End:	Interest on 24,271.82	728.16
Total fund		24,999.98

Or the accumulation may be shown as follows:

SINKING FUND TABLE

Year	Contribution	Interest	Total
1	5,801.62	174.05	5,975.67
2	5,801.62	353.32	12,130.61
3	5,801.62	537.97	8,470.20
4	5,801.62	728.16	24,999.98
Total	23,206.48	1,793.50	

INTERIM INTEREST DATES

Sometimes the interest is compounded more frequently than the rents are payable. For instance, the rents of the annuity may be due annually, while the interest may be compounded semi-annually or quarterly. Such a problem offers no difficulty if one remembers that the nominal and effective rates per annum differ under such conditions.

Illustration: what is the amount of an annuity of four rents of $100.00 each, payable at the expiration of a year, if the rents are invested at 6% per annum compounded semi-annually?

Although the rate is stated as 6% per annum, it is really 3% a half year. The ratio of increase each half year is, therefore, 1.03, and the ratio of increase each year is 1.03^2, or 1.0609. Hence the effective rate per annum is 6.09%.

The amount of 1 for four years at 3% a half year, is 1.03^8, or 1.266770; hence the compound interest is .266770. The amount of an annuity of 1 is computed as follows:

$$s_{\overline{4}|} = .266770 \div .0609$$
$$= 4.38046$$

And the amount of an annuity of 100 is 438.05.

The following table is set up by way of proof:

ACCUMULATION OF ANNUITY

First Year:
    End: Contribution: 100.00

Second Year:

Middle:	Interest on 100.00	3.00	
End:	" " 103.00	3.09	6.09
	Contribution		100.00
	Total		206.09

Third Year:

Middle:	Interest on 206.09	6.18	
End:	" " 212.27	6.37	12.55
	Contribution		100.00
	Total		318.64

Fourth Year:

Middle:	Interest on 318.64	9.56	
End:	" " 328.20	9.85	19.41
	Contribution		100.00
	Total (as above)		438.05

If the rents are payable at the beginning of each year the amount is first computed for a similar annuity in which the rents are due at the end of each year, and this amount is multiplied by the ratio of increase.

Illustration: Assuming that each of the $100.00 rents in the preceding illustration was payable at the beginning of the year, what would be the amount of the annuity at the end of the fourth year?

	438.05	amount of annuity when rents are payable at end
Multiply by	1.0609	
	464.73	amount of annuity when rents are payable at beginning

The following table is set up in proof:

ACCUMULATION OF ANNUITY

First Year:

Beginning:	Contribution	100.00
Middle:	Interest on 100.00	3.00
End:	" " 103.00	3.09
Total		106.09

Second Year:

Beginning:	Contribution	100.00
Middle:	Interest on 206.09	6.18
End:	" " 212.27	6.37
Total		218.64

Third Year:

Beginning:	Contribution	100.00
Middle:	Interest on 318.64	9.56
End:	" " 328.20	9.85
Total		338.05

Fourth Year:

Beginning:	Contribution	100.00
Middle:	Interest on 438.05	13.14
End:	" " 451.19	13.54
Total (as above)		464.73

The accumulation of interest at interim dates finds application in sinking funds which are accumulated by annual deposits, while the interest on the fund is compounded semi-annually. This is ordinarily the case with sinking funds, because the contributions are usually made annually, and the funds are invested in bonds bearing coupons payable semi-annually. To find the periodical contributions which will produce the required fund, compute the amount of an annuity of 1 by the process described in the preceding paragraph and divide the required fund by this amount.

Computing an Unknown Rate

When the rents, the amount and the time of an annuity are known, it may be desired to compute the rate, as in the following illustration:

At what rate will an ordinary annuity of four rents of $100.00 amount to $418.36?

Problems of this nature are impossible of exact solution. Working with the formula for the amount of an annuity,

$$s_{\overline{n}|} = I \div i$$

we know the value of $s_{\overline{n}|}$, which in this case is 4.1836. The value of I is unknown, but substituting for I its equivalent $(1+i)^n - 1$, in which the value of n is known to be 4, the knowns and unknowns can be stated as follows:

$$4.1836 = \frac{(1+i)^4 - 1}{i}$$

This equation cannot be solved to obtain an exact value of i. Perhaps the best method of obtaining an approximation is by reference to a table showing amounts of annuities. A table shows the following amounts at various rates for four periods:

Periods	2%	2½%	3%	3½%	4%
4	4.121608	4.152516	4.183627	4.214943	4.246464

This table shows that the required rate is 3%. But assume that the table does not show this rate, and that the amounts nearest to the 4.1836 stated in the problem are

	Rates	Amounts
at	3½%	4.214943
"	2½%	4.152516
differences	1 %	.062427

Then a difference of 1% in the rate causes a difference of .062427 in the amount.

The amount at the unknown rate is   4.1836
and the amount at the next lower known rate is 4.152516
and the difference is   .031084

If an increase of .062427 in the amount is caused by an increase of 1% in the rate, the increase of .031084 in the amount is caused by an increase in the rate of approximately

$$\frac{0.31084}{.062427} \text{ of } 1\%.$$

.031084 ÷ .062427 = .498

Hence the approximate rate is 2.5% + .498%, or 2.998%, which is very close to the true rate of 3%.

Computing an Unknown Time

When the rents, the amount and the rate of an annuity are known, the unknown number of periods can be computed by logarithms.

Illustration: in how many periods will rents of $100.00 amount to $418.36 at 3%?

Dividing $418.36 by 100, the amount of an annuity of 1 is determined as 4.1836.

Applying the formula $s_{\overline{n}|} = I \div i$, or

$$s_{\overline{n}|} = \frac{(1+i)^n - 1}{i}$$

the knowns and unknowns are

$$4.1836 = \frac{1.03^n - 1}{.03}$$

Multiplying both sides by .03 $\qquad 4.1836 \times .03 = 1.03^n - 1$

or $\qquad\qquad\qquad\qquad\qquad .125508 = 1.03^n - 1$

adding 1 to both sides $\qquad\quad 1.125508 = 1.03^n$

Then by logarithms:

$$\text{log. } 1.125508 = \text{log. } 103 \times n$$

and $\qquad \dfrac{\text{log. } 1.125508}{\text{log. } 1.03} = n$

log. 1.125508 is .051346

log. 1.03 is .012837

.051346 ÷ .012837 = 4, the number of periods.

Since 1.125508 is the amount of 1 for n periods at the known rate, and since 1.03 is the ratio of increase, $1+i$, the formula for computing the time required to produce a known amount of an annuity may be stated

$$n = \frac{\text{log. S}}{\text{log. } (1+i)}$$

PRESENT VALUE OF ANNUITY

The present value of an annuity is the sum which must be put at interest to produce the desired rents. This invested sum is increased by the interest accretions and decreased by the payment of the rents, the balance remaining at the date when the last rent is due being exactly sufficient to provide for the last rent.

Illustration: a contract requires the payment of $100.00 on December 31, 1916, and each year thereafter until December 31, 1919. What sum invested at 3% per annum one year before the first $100.00 payment is due will be sufficient to provide the four payments?

Clearly the sum will be less than $400.00 because of the interest. The present value of each of the four rents may be computed, and the sum of these present values will be the present value of the annuity. Thus:

Rent due	Rent	Periods present value earns interest	Present value at 3%
Dec. 31, 1916	100.00	1	97.0874
" 31, 1917	100.00	2	94.2596
" 31, 1918	100.00	3	91.5142
" 31, 1919	100.00	4	88.8487
Present value of four rents			371.7099

When the present value of an annuity is computed in this manner, the present value of the first rent may be computed by dividing the rent by the ratio of increase $(1+i)$. This present value is divided by the ratio of increase to determine the present value of the second rent; the quotient of each division serves as the dividend for the next succeeding division, thus:

```
100.00   ÷1.03 =97.0874 present value of rent due 1 period hence
 97.0874÷1.03 =94.2596    "      "  "   "   " 2 periods  "
 94.2596÷1.03 =91.5142    "      "  "   "   " 3    "     "
 91.5142÷1.03 =88.8487    "      "  "   "   " 4    "     "
              ─────────
              371.7099 present value of the annuity
```

This method is too laborious to be employed when there are many rents, and the labor can be avoided by applying the following short method:

To compute the present value of an annuity of 1 for a given number of periods at a given rate, divide the compound discount on 1 for the same number of periods at the given rate by the interest rate. Representing the present value of an ordinary or immediate annuity of 1 per period for n periods by the symbol $a_{\overline{n}|}$,

$$a_{\overline{n}|} = D \div i$$

Applying this formula to the illustration, the first step is to determine the compound discount, D. A table of present values of 1 shows .888487 as the present value of 1 at 3% due four periods hence.

Then $1 - .888487 = .111513$, the compound discount; and $.111513 \div .03 = 3.7171$ the present value of an annuity of 1; and $3.7171 \times 100 = 371.71$ the present value of an annuity of 100.

The reduction of this present value may be tabulated as follows:

December 31, 1915	Present value	371.71
December 31, 1916	Interest at 3% on 371.71	11.15
	Total	382.86
	Rent deducted	100.00
	Balance	282.86
December 31, 1917	Interest at 3% on 282.86	8.49
	Total	291.35
	Rent deducted	100.00
	Balance	191.35
December 31, 1918	Interest at 3% on 191.35	5.74
	Total	197.09
	Rent deducted	100.00
	Balance	97.09
December 31, 1919	Interest at 3% on 97.09	2.91
	Total	100.00
	Rent deducted	100.00
	Balance	0.00

Or thus:

SCHEDULE OF REDUCTION OF ANNUITY

Date	Interest added	Rent deducted	Balance
Dec. 31, 1915			371.71
" 31, 1916	11.15	100.00	282.86
" 31, 1917	8.49	100.00	191.35
" 31, 1918	5.74	100.00	97.09
" 31, 1919	2.91	100.00	0.00
	28.29	400.00	

Interest books usually contain tables showing present values of annuities, in the following form:

PRESENT VALUE OF ANNUITY OF 1

Periods	3%	3½%	4%	4½%	5%
1	.970874	.966184	.961538	.956938	.952381
2	1.913470	1.899694	1.886095	1.872668	1.859410
3	2.828611	2.801637	2.775091	2.748964	2.723248
4	3.717098	3.673079	3.629895	3.587526	3.545951
5	4.579707	4.515052	4.451822	4.389977	4.329477
6	5.417191	5.328553	5.242137	5.157872	5.075692
7	6.230283	6.114544	6.002055	5.892701	5.786373
8	7.019692	6.873956	6.732745	6.595886	6.463213

In the absence of such a table, the present value of an annuity can be computed by repeated divisions to determine the present value of each successive rent, as illustrated above, or by applying the formula $a_{\overline{n}|} = D \div i$. If a table of present values of 1 is available, the value of D can be obtained by subtraction, thus:

1.00
.888487 present value of 1 at 3% for 4 periods.
_____
.111513 compound discount at 3% for 4 periods.

If one has only a table of amounts of 1, the value of D can be computed by applying the formula $D = I \div S$, thus: The table of amounts of 1 shows:

$$1.03^4 = 1.125509$$
Then $.125509 \div 1.125509 = .111513$

PRESENT VALUE OF ANNUITY DUE

If the rents are payable at the beginning of each period, no interest will be earned on the invested sum before withdrawing the first rent. Therefore it will be necessary to invest a larger sum than would be invested if the annuity were an ordinary one. If the present value of an ordinary annuity for the same number of periods is known, the present value of an annuity due may be computed by a method based on the following reasoning:

The extra amount to be invested is equal to the interest earned on the present value of an ordinary annuity during the first period. Therefore, the present value of an annuity due can be computed by multiplying the present value of an ordinary annuity of the same number of rents at the same rate, by $1+i$, the ratio of increase.

Illustration: what sum must be invested on January 1, 1916, to permit the withdrawal of four rents of $100.00 each on the first day of January, 1916, 1917, 1918 and 1919? Interest at 3% a year.

This is an annuity due of 4 rents at 3%. The present value of an ordinary annuity of 4 rents of 1 at 3% was computed in the preceding illustration. It is 3.717099. Then 3.717099×1.03 = 3.828612, the present value of an annuity due of 1. And 3.828612 ×100 = 382.86, the present value of an annuity due of 100.

The reduction of this present value may be shown thus:

January 1, 1916	Present value	$382.86
	Rent deducted	100.00
	Balance	282.86
January 1, 1917	Interest at 3% on $282.86	8.49
	Total	291.35
	Rent deducted	100.00
	Balance	191.35
January 1, 1918	Interest at 3% on $191.35	5.74
	Total	197.09
	Rent deducted	100.00
	Balance	97.09
January 1, 1919	Interest at 3% on $97.09	2.91
	Total	100.00
	Rent deducted	100.00
	Balance	0.00

The present value of the annuity due for four periods is the sum of the first rent plus the present value of the last three rents. Therefore, when a table of present values of ordinary annuities is available, take the present value of such an annuity for $n-1$ periods and add one rent

To illustrate: the annuity table shows

2.828611 present value of ordinary annuity of 3 rents at 3%
Add 1.000000

3.828611 present value of annuity due of 4 rents at 3%

I 1

INTERIM INTEREST DATES

In cases where the time between the withdrawals of rents is divided into smaller interest periods, as in an annuity where the interest is compounded semi-annually and the rents are withdrawn, annually, consideration must be given to the difference between the nominal and the effective interest rates.

Illustration: what sum invested at 6% a year, interest compounded semi-annually, will produce four rents of $100.00, drawn annually, the first withdrawal being made one year after investing the present value of the annuity?

With eight interest periods and a rate of 3% per period, the first step in the solution is to find the present value of 1 due 8 periods hence at 3%. This is shown by a table of present values to be .789409. Then the compound discount is .210591.

The effective rate per year is computed thus:

$$1.03^2 = 1.0609 \text{ ratio of increase per annum.}$$

And 6.09% is the effective rate per annum.

Then .210591÷.0609=3.45798 present value of annuity of 1.

3.45798×100=345.80 present value of annuity of 100.

The reduction of this annuity may be shown thus:

345'8 + 10'37

First year:

Beginning:	Investment	345.80
Middle:	Interest at 3% on $345.80	10.37
End:	" " " " 356.17	10.69
	Total	366.86
	Rent withdrawn	100.00
	Balance	266.86

Second year:

Middle:	Interest at 3% on 266.86		8.01
End:	" " " " 274.87		8.25

Total	283.12
Rent withdrawn	100.00
Balance	183.12

Third year:

Middle:	Interest at 3% on 183.12		5.49
End:	" " " " 188.61		5.66

Total	194.27
Rent withdrawn	100.00
Balance	94.27

Fourth year:

Middle:	Interest at 3% on 94.27		2.83
End:	" " " " 97.10		2.91

Total	100.01
Rent withdrawn	100.01
Balance	0.00

→ Rejected → refused

PRESENT VALUE OF DEFERRED ANNUITY

A deferred annuity is one which does not begin to run until after the expiration of a number of periods. For instance, an annuity of 5 rents deferred 10 periods is one which does not begin to run until after the expiration of 10 periods. If the periods are a year in length, ten years will elapse before the first period in which a payment is to be made, and as the rents are ordinarily due at the ends of periods, the first rent will not be due until the end of the eleventh year.

a la llegada de Duración

To illustrate the method of computing the present value of such an annuity, assume that the 5 rents are $500 each, the annuity being deferred ten periods. The present value at 5% a year is desired.

The rents are payable at the end of the 11th, 12th, 13th, 14th and 15th years. If we were required to find the present value of the annuity at the beginning of the 11th year, the solution would consist merely of computing the present value of an ordinary annuity of 5 rents, as follows:

Present value of 1 at 5% in 5 periods = .783526
Compound discount   .216474
.216474 ÷ .05 = 4.32948 present value of ordinary annuity of 1.

Sumplement Just, only

By investing 4.32948 at the beginning of the 11th year it will be possible to draw out rents of 1 at each rent date. But since the annuity is deferred 10 periods the investment, made at the beginning of the first year, will earn interest for 10 periods before the beginning of the 11th year. Then if 4.32948 invested at the beginning of the 11th period will produce the annuity, the investment at the beginning of the first year need be only the present value of 4.32948.

Present value of 1 at 5% in 10 periods = .613913
Multiply by   4.32948
Present value deferred annuity of 1   2.65792
Multiply by   500
Present value of deferred annuity of 500 1328.96

The method of procedure may be stated thus: to find the present value of an annuity of 1 for n periods deferred m periods, compute the value of an ordinary annuity of 1 for n periods and multiply by the present value of 1 due m periods hence. Proof of the accuracy of 1328.96:

This investment earns compound interest for 11 years before the first rent is withdrawn:

$$1.05^{11} = 1.710339$$

Multiply by 1328.96

	2,272.97	
Deduct 1st rent	500.00	
	1,772.97	value end of 11th year
Add 5% interest	88.65	
	1,861.62	
Deduct 2nd rent	500.00	
	1,361.62	" " " 12th "
Add 5% interest	68.08	
	1,429.70	
Deduct 3rd rent	500.00	
	929.70	" " " 13th "
Add 5% interest	46.49	
	976.19	
Deduct 4th rent	500.00	
	476.19	" " " 14th "
Add 5% interest	23.81	
	500.00	
Deduct 5th rent	500.00	
	0.00	" " " 15th "

RENTS PRODUCED BY KNOWN PRESENT VALUE

An annuity problem of frequent application is the determination of rents produced by a known present value. To illustrate: if $5,000.00

is invested at 5% a year, what rents can be withdrawn at the end of each of 10 years?

If it were desired to withdraw rents of $1, the present value of
an annuity of 1 for 10 periods at 5% would be invested. This
present value could be determined from an interest table, or
computed. It is 7.721735.

Then 5,000÷7.721735=647.52 annual rent produced by investment of $5,000.

Hence to find the rents, divide the investment or
known present value by the present value of an
annuity of 1 for *n* periods at the rate *i*.

EQUAL INSTALMENTS IN PAYMENT OF A DEBT

The procedure explained above is used to
compute the equal periodical amounts to be paid
in settlement of the principal and interest of a
debt.

To illustrate: assume that A borrows $5,000.00
from B at 5% and agrees to pay principal and
interest in ten equal annual instalments, the first
instalment to be paid at the expiration of one
year. These ten payments are an annuity, and
if A invested the $5,000.00 at 5% it would, of
course, exactly provide the annual amounts
which he could draw out and pay to B.

Since $5,000.00 is the present value of 10 unknown rents
at 5%, and since 7.721735 is the present value of 10 rents of 1
at 5%

5,000.00÷7.721735=647.52 the equal instalment.

The reduction of the debt may be shown as follows:

ANNUITY REPAYMENT OF DEBT

Year	Total (+)	Payment Of interest (—)	Payment On principal (—)	Balance of principal
				5000.00
1	(647.52) = (250.00	+	397.52)	4602.48
2	647.52	230.12	417.40	4185.08
3	647.52	209.25	438.27	3746.81
4	647.52	187.34	460.18	3286.63
5	647.52	164.33	483.19	2803.44
6	647.52	140.17	507.35	2296.09
7	647.52	114.80	532.72	1763.37
8	647.52	88.17	559.35	1204.02
9	647.52	60.20	587.32	616.70
10	647.52	30.83	616.69	.01
	6475.20	1475.21	4999.99	

LEASEHOLD PREMIUMS

When the rental value of real estate has increased, the holder of a lease may prefer to sublet rather than to continue to occupy the property. If so, he takes as his gain the difference between the rent he pays on the original lease and the rent he receives on the sub-lease.

For instance, A owns property which he has leased to B for 20 years at $3,000.00 a year, payable in advance. At the expiration of the seventh year C wishes to occupy the property and is willing to pay $4,000.00 a year for it. Several different arrangements may be made.

B may sub-lease to C, collecting $4,000.00 a year, and paying $3,000.00 to A. C may pay $3,000.00 to A and $1,000.00 to B each year. He may pay A $3,000.00 a year, and pay B the present value of the thirteen payments of $1,000.00 each. The present value of these $1,000.00 payments is the premium paid for the lease.

Since the rent is payable in advance, the first rent is due. The premium to be paid is the present value of an annuity due of 13 rents. If B and C agree on 5% as the rate for discounting the annuity, the computation of the premium would be as follows:

.530321 = present value of 1 due 13 periods hence at 5%
.469678 ÷ .05 = 9.39356, present value or ordinary annuity of 1
9.39356 × 1000 = 9,393.56, present value of ordinary annuity of 1000
9,393.56 × 1.05 = 9,863.24, present value of annuity due of 1000.

Or as follows:

8.863252, present value of ordinary annuity of 1 at 5% for 12 periods, as shown by annuity table.
8.863252 × 1000 = 8,863.252 present value of ordinary annuity of 1000
8,863.25 + 1000 = 9,863.25 present value of annuity due of 1000 for 13 periods.

C would charge this 9,863.25 to leasehold premium, and would write it off as scheduled below:

REDUCTION OF LEASEHOLD PREMIUM

Year	Debit rent	Credit interest	Credit leasehold premium	Balance
				9,863.25
1	1,000.00		1,000.00	8,863.25
2	1,000.00	443.16	556.84	8,306.41
3	1,000.00	415.32	584.68	7,721.73
4	1,000.00	386.09	613.91	7,107.82
5	1,000.00	355.39	644.61	6,463.21
6	1,000.00	323.16	676.84	5,786.37
7	1,000.00	289.32	710.68	5,075.69
8	1,000.00	253.79	746.21	4,329.48
9	1,000.00	216.47	783.53	3,545.95
10	1,000.00	177.30	822.70	2,723.25
11	1,000.00	136.16	863.84	1,859.41
12	1,000.00	92.97	907.03	952.38
13	1,000.00	47.62	952.38	
Total	13,000.00	3,136.75	9,863.25	

If the rents had been payable at the end of each year and the transfer of the lease had been made at the beginning of the year, the computation of the premium would be a problem of the present value of an ordinary annuity instead of the present value of an annuity due.

BOND PRICES

The price at which a bond will sell is affected by the nominal interest rate, the mortgaged security, the financial standing of the issuing company and the probability of being able to sell the bond if occasion requires.

Bonds rarely sell on the market at par—usually a premium is added or a discount deducted.

Quotations are made "on a basis" or "at a price." When bonds are sold at a price other than par the effective interest rate differs from the nominal or coupon rate. Thus if a bond is issued at a discount, the principal borrowed is really less than par. Moreover, the borrower pays not only the interest coupons but also the discount for the use of the borrowed money. Hence the effective rate on the loan is greater than the nominal rate. If the bond sells at a premium, the principal borrowed is more than par; and since the borrower does not have to pay back the premium at maturity, the premium is really a deduction from the interest. Hence the effective rate is less than the nominal rate.

Quotations "on a basis" state the effective rate to be earned. The price, above or below par, may then be found in a bond table, or computed. Thus a 5 year 6% bond of $100.00 bought on a 5% basis would cost $104.38 as shown in the following table—or a 5 year 5% bond of $100.00 bought on a 6% basis would cost $95.73.

ILLUSTRATION OF A BOND TABLE

Per cent. per annum

	3%	3½%	4%	4½%	5%	6%	7%
		5 years—Interest payable semi-annually					
4.75	92.29	94.49	96.70	98.90	101.10	105.51	109.91
4.80	92.08	94.28	96.48	98.68	100.88	105.28	109.58
4.875	91.77	93.96	96.16	98.35	100.55	104.94	109.33
4.90	91.66	93.86	96.05	98.25	100.44	104.83	109.21

ILLUSTRATION OF A BOND TABLE—Cont.

Per cent.   5 years—Interest payable semi-annually

per annum	3%	3½%	4%	4½%	5%	6%	7%
5.	91.25	93.44	95.62	97.81	100.00	104.38	108.75
5.10	90.83	93.02	95.20	97.38	99.56	103.93	108.29
5.125	90.73	92.91	95.09	97.27	99.45	103.82	108.18
5.20	90.42	92.60	94.78	96.95	99.13	103.48	107.84
5.25	90.22	92.39	94.57	96.74	98.91	103.26	107.61
5.30	90.01	92.18	94.35	96.53	98.70	103.04	107.38
5.375	89.71	91.87	94.04	96.21	98.37	102.71	107.04
5.40	89.61	91.77	93.94	96.10	98.27	102.60	106.93
5.50	89.20	91.36	93.52	95.68	97.84	102.16	106.48
5.625	88.70	90.85	93.00	95.16	97.31	101.61	105.92
5.75	88.20	90.34	92.49	94.63	96.78	101.07	105.37
5.875	87.70	89.84	91.98	94.12	96.26	100.53	104.81
6.	87.20	89.34	91.47	93.60	95.73	100.00	104.27

COMPUTING THE PREMIUM

When the effective rate is less than the nominal rate, the premium may be computed by a method based on the following reasoning:

Assume that the par of the bond is $1,000.00, the time 5 years, the nominal rate 6% a year payable semi-annually, and that the bond is to be purchased on a 5% basis. The conditions are such that the purchaser is satisfied with 5% a year; therefore, if the bond bore coupons of 2½% or $25.00 payable each six months the bond would presumably sell at par. In other words, the purchaser would pay par, $1,000.00, for the right to receive par at maturity and interest of $25.00 semi-annually. But since the coupons are $30.00

each, he must also pay for the right to receive this extra $5.00 each six months. This semi-annual payment of $5.00 is an annuity, and the purchaser will pay its present value discounted at the effective interest rate of 2½% per period thus:

.781198 = present value of 1 @ 2½% in 10 periods
.218802 ÷ .025 = 8.75208 present value of annuity of 1
8.75208 × 5 = 43.76040 present value of annuity of 5, the premium.

The method may be stated as follows:

Compute the interest for 1 period at the nominal rate on par $30.00
"   "   "   " 1 "   " " effective " " "   25.00

Find the difference, which is one rent of an annuity   5.00

Find the present value of this annuity at the effective rate.

Another method of computing the cost of a bond at a premium is based on the following reasoning:

The purchaser will pay the present value of the benefits to be received, which are ordinarily:

Par at maturity;
The interest coupons.

The present value of these benefits will be computed at the effective rate. Applied to the preceding illustration, the computation by this method would be:

Present value of par:
      .781198, present value of 1 due 10 periods hence at 2½%
      .781198×1000=   781.198

Present value of coupons:
      .218802 (compound discount)÷.025=8.75208
                present value of annuity of 1
      30.00 (coupons) × 8.75208=   262.562

Total (as computed above)   1,043.760

The interest and amortization of premium on this bond may be scheduled as follows:

AMORTIZATION—BOND AT A PREMIUM

Cost					1,043.76
1st interest date:		Coupon	30.00		
		Interest: 2½% of 1043.76	26.09		3.91
		Carrying value			1,039.85
2nd " "		Coupon	30.00		
		Interest: 2½% of 1039.85	26.00		4.00
		Carrying value			1,035.85
3rd " "		Coupon	30.00		
		Interest: 2½% of 1035.85	25.90		4.10
		Carrying value			1,031.75
4th " "		Coupon	30.00		
		Interest: 2½% of 1031.75	25.79		4.21
		Carrying value			1,027.54
5th " "		Coupon	30.00		
		Interest: 2½% of 1027.54	25.69		4.31
		Carrying value			1,023.23
6th " "		Coupon	30.00		
		Interest: 2½% of 1023.23	25.58		4.42
		Carrying value			1,018.81

7th interest date:	Coupon	30.00	
	Interest: 2½% of 1018.81	25.47	4.53
	Carrying value		1,014.28
8th " "	Coupon	30.00	
	Interest: 2½% of 1014.28	25.36	4.64
	Carrying value		1,009.64
9th " "	Coupon	30.00	
	Interest: 2½% of 1009.64	25.24	4.76
	Carrying value		1,004.88
10th " "	Coupon	30.00	
	Interest: 2½% of 1004.88	25.12	4.88
	Par—payable at maturity		1,000.00

Or the schedule may be shown thus:

AMORTIZATION—BOND AT A PREMIUM

End of period	Coupon	Effective interest	Premium written off	Carrying value
				1,043.76
	30.00	26.09	3.91	1,039.85
2	30.00	26.00	4.00	1,035.85
3	30.00	25.90	4.10	1,031.75
4	30.00	25.79	4.21	1,027.54
5	30.00	25.69	4.31	1,023.23
6	30.00	25.58	4.42	1,018.81
7	30.00	25.47	4.53	1,014.28
8	30.00	25.36	4.64	1,009.64
9	30.00	25.24	4.76	1,004.88
10	30.00	25.12	4.88	1,000.00
	300.00	256.24	43.76	

The second method of computing the price, described above, is the better one to use when bonds are repayable at a premium.

Illustration: what price, to net 5%, should be paid for a 5½% twenty-year bond of $1,000.00, repayable with a bonus of 5%?

Present value of 1050 due at maturity:

.3724306, present value of 1 at 2½% in 40 periods
.3724306×1050=   391.052

Present value of coupons:

.6275694÷.025=25.102776 present value of
                                    annuity of 1
25.102776×27.50=   690.326

Total   ·   1,081.378

COMPUTING THE DISCOUNT

The two methods described for computing the price of a bond sold at a premium may also be used when the bond is sold at a discount.

To illustrate: at what price should a $1,000.00 5 year 5% bond be sold to net the investor 6%? Interest is payable semi-annually.

By the first method the difference between the interest on par at the effective rate and at the nominal rate is computed—the discount is the present value of an annuity for the number of interest periods, each rent of which is the difference in the interest at the two rates. This annuity is discounted at the effective interest rate.

Effective rate: 3% on 1,000=	30.00
Nominal rate: 2½% on 1,000=	25.00
Difference:	5.00

.744094 is the present value of 1 at 3% due 10 periods hence:
.255906÷.03=8.5302 present value of annuity of 1.
8.5302×5=42.6510, the discount.
1,000.00−42.65=957.35, the price.

By the second method the present values of par and coupons are computed at the effective rate:

Present value of par:

.744094×1000=	744.094

Present value of coupons:
.255906÷.03=8.5302

8.5302×25=	213.255
Total:	957.349

The reduction of this discount may be scheduled thus:

SCHEDULE OF AMORTIZATION—BOND AT DISCOUNT

First period:

Cost:		957.35
Interest: 3% of 957.35	28.72	
Coupon	25.00	3.72
Carrying value		961.07

Second period:

Interest: 3% of 961.07	28.83	
Coupon	25.00	3.83
Carrying value		964.90

Third period:

Interest: 3% of 964.90	28.95	
Coupon	25.00	3.95
Carrying value		968.85

Fourth period:

Interest: 3% of 968.85	29.07	
Coupon	25.00	4.07
Carrying value		972.92

Fifth period:

Interest: 3% of 972.92	29.19	
Coupon	25.00	4.19
Carrying value		977.11

Sixth period:

Interest: 3% of 977.11	29.31	
Coupon	25.00	4.31
Carrying value		981.42

Seventh period:

Interest: 3% of 981.42	29.44	
Coupon	25.00	4.44
Carrying value		985.86

Eighth period:

Interest: 3% of 985.86	29.58	
Coupon	25.00	4.58
Carrying value		990.44

Ninth period:

Interest: 3% of 990.44	29.71	
Coupon	25.00	4.71
Carrying value		995.15

Tenth period:

Interest: 3% of 995.15	29.85	
Coupon	25.00	4.85
Carrying value		1000.00

Or thus:

SCHEDULE OF AMORTIZATION

Period	Effective interest	Coupon	Discount	Carrying value
				957.35
1	28.72	25.00	3.72	961.07
2	28.83	25.00	3.83	964.90
3	28.95	25.00	3.95	968.85
4	29.07	25.00	4.07	972.92
5	29.19	25.00	4.19	977.11
6	29.31	25.00	4.31	981.42
7	29.44	25.00	4.44	985.86
8	29.58	25.00	4.58	990.44
9	29.71	25.00	4.71	995.15
10	29.85	25.00	4.85	1000.00
Total	292.65	250.00	42.65	

PURCHASES AT INTERMEDIATE DATES

When bonds are sold between interest dates, the customary method of computing the price is as follows:

Determine the price which would have been paid at the last preceding interest date. Determine the price which would have been paid at the next succeeding interest date. Find the difference between these prices. This difference is the premium or discount which would be amortized for the entire period in which the purchase was made.

Determine the fraction of the period expired between the last preceding interest date and the date of purchase.

Multiply the difference in prices (premium or discount for whole period) by the fraction of the period expired. The product is the premium or discount for the fractional period.

Deduct such premium for the fractional period from the price at the last preceding interest date, or add the discount for the fractional period.

To the result thus obtained add the accrued interest on par at the nominal rate.

Illustration—bond at premium: what price should be paid for a $100.00 bond due in 6 years and 2 months, bearing 6% and bought on a 5% basis plus accrued interest?

Value 6½ years to maturity (per bond table)	105.49
" 6 " " " " " " .	105.13
Difference—premium amortized in 6 months	.36
Multiply by fraction of period expired—4 months	⅔
Premium amortized in 4 months	.24
Price 6½ years to maturity	105.49
Deduct premium for 4 months	.24
Value 6 years, 2 months before maturity (flat)	105.25
Interest for 4 months on $100.00 at 6%	2.00
Price including interest	107.25

At the next interest date the bond will be written down to $105.13, its value at that date as shown by the bond table.

Illustration—bond at a discount: what price should be paid for a $100.00 bond due in 8 years and 1 month, bearing 4% and bought on a 5½% basis plus accrued interest?

Value 8 years to maturity (per bond table)	90.40
" 8½ " " " " " "	89.92
Difference—discount amortized in 6 months	.48
Multiply by fraction of period expired—5 months	5/6
Discount amortized in 5 months	.40
Add value 8½ years before maturity	89.92
Add accrued interest at 4% on $100 for 5 months	1.67
Price including interest	91.99

Optional Redemption

When a bond or other obligation gives the debtor the option of paying the debt before maturity, this right must be taken into consideration in determining the price to be paid if the purchase is to be made at a premium or a discount.

If the debtor has the right to redeem at par before maturity, the purchase price should be computed on the assumption that the right will be exercised if the bond is purchased at a premium. The reason for the assumption can be shown by a comparison of prices in a bond table.

A 6% bond payable in 20 years bought on a 5% basis should cost 112.55

A 6% bond payable in 15 years bought on a 5% basis should cost 110.47.

Now if the bond is payable in twenty years with an option to redeem in fifteen years the purchaser may be buying a bond with only fifteen years to run; and he should pay for it on the supposition that it will be paid at the optional date.

On the other hand if the bond is to be purchased at a discount, he should assume that it will not be paid until maturity. A bond table shows that a 5% bond payable in 15 years bought on a 6% basis should cost 90.20; a 5% bond payable in 20 years bought on a 6% basis should cost 88.44.

If the purchaser pays 90.20 for the bond and it is not paid for twenty years, he will not earn 6% on his investment. In fact, he will earn a little less than $5\frac{1}{8}\%$.

If the debtor must pay a premium in order to redeem the bond before maturity, the purchaser should assume that the option will not be exercised in case the bond is to be sold at a discount. It was shown in the preceding paragraph that a 5% bond sold on a 6% basis would sell for $90.20 if redeemable at par at the end of 15 years. If redeemable at a premium, it would sell for a still higher price. But a purchaser would be unwise to pay this higher price when there is a possibility that the bond will run the full twenty years. He should buy on the assumption that the option will not be exercised. If it is exercised his rate of earning will be more than 6%.

But if the bond is to be purchased at a premium, and if the debtor must pay a premium to redeem the bond before maturity, the purchaser cannot assume that the option will be exercised, nor can he assume that it will not be exercised. The advantage to the debtor arising from the payment at par, on an optional maturity date may vanish if he has to pay a premium if he redeems before maturity. Whether or not it will be advantageous will depend on the amount of the premium. Therefore, the purchaser should compute the price to be paid on the given basis if the bond runs to maturity, and the price to be paid if the option to redeem at a premium is exercised; and he should then pay the lower price.

To illustrate: on a 5% basis what should be paid for a $1,000.00 6% bond, due in 20 years, with a privilege of redemption in 15 years at 110?

A bond table shows the value on a 5% basis of a 20 year 6% bond to be $1,125.50.

The value if the option is exercised could be computed thus:

Value of 1,100 in 15 years:
    Present value of 1 at 2½% due 30 periods hence. .476742685
    Multiply by   1100
                                         ———————
                                   524.4169535

Value of coupons:
  Present value of 1, as above   .476742685
  Compound discount   .523257315
  .523257315÷.02½=20.9302926, present value of annuity
                      of 1
         20.9302926×30=627.908778
Value of par and premium   524.4169
Value of coupons   627.9087

Total   1152.3256

The price, on the assumption that the bond runs to maturity, is $1,125.50. On the assumption that it is paid at the optional date, the price is $1,152.33. The purchaser should assume that the option will not be exercised and pay $1,125.50.

If the premium to be paid at the optional redemption date is not too large, it may still be desirable to exercise the option.

To illustrate: what price should be paid for the bond in the preceding illustration if the optional redemption price is 101 instead of 110? Price if option is not exercised: $1,125.50, as above.

Price if option is exercised:

Present value of 1010 in 15 years:
  Present value of 1 at 2½% due 30 periods hence .476742685
  Multiply by   1010

                                                 481.5101
Present value of coupons—as above   627.9087

Total   1,109.4188

This price, $1,109.42, should be paid because it is less than $1,125.50.

COMPUTING THE RATE ON BONDS SOLD AT PREMIUM OR DISCOUNT

When a bond is purchased on the basis of an effective rate other than the nominal rate, it is a simple matter to compute the price to be paid; but when the bond is purchased at a price not listed in the bond tables, it is by no means an easy matter to compute the price. In fact, there is no mathematical formula which can be applied to determine the rate exactly. The rate can be approximated in several ways, two of which will be explained.

A 25 year 6% $100 bond, interest payable semi-annually, is purchased for $110.38. What is the effective rate?

This price of $110.38 is shown by a bond table to be the price on a 5.25% basis. The bond table shows:

25 years 6%

5.20%	111.12
5.25	110.38
5.30	109.64]

But let us assume that the 110.38 is not shown by the table and that the nearest values are

On a 5.20 basis	111.12
On a 5.30 "	109.64

Then .10 of one per cent. difference in the rate causes 1.48 difference in price.

Price on a 5.20 basis	111.12
Price given in illustration	110.38
Difference	.74

Then to find the approximate rate, add to 5.20%

$$\frac{74}{148} \text{ of } .10 \text{ of } 1\%$$

$$\frac{74}{148} \text{ of } .10 = .05$$

$$5.20\% + .05\% = 5.25\% \text{ the rate.}$$

This rate happens to be exactly correct, but it is very unusual to obtain exact results by interpolation.

The rate may be approximated by the following formulas when bond tables are not available for interpolation:—

Bond at a premium:

$$r = \frac{2\,(I - Pr)}{n\left(C + P + \dfrac{Pr}{n}\right)}$$

Bond at a discount:

$$r = \frac{2\,(I + D)}{n\left(C + P - \dfrac{D}{n}\right)}$$

The symbols used are:

r—effective rate per period
P—par
I—total interest on bonds
Pr—premium
D—discount
C—cost (par + premium; or par — discount).
n—number of interest periods.

Applying the first formula to the illustration:

$$r = \frac{2\,(150 - 10.38)}{50\left(110.38 + 100 + \dfrac{10.38}{50}\right)} = 2.65\% \text{ per period}$$

or 5.30% per annum.

It will be noted that this result is much less exact than the one obtained by interpolation—still it is useful when one has no bond table and desires to obtain a rough approximation of the rate.

Illustration of bond at a discount: a 10 year 5% $100 bond is bought at 96.94. Interest payable semi-annually. What is the approximate effective rate?

$$r = \frac{2\,(50 + 3.06)}{20\left(96.94 + 100 - \dfrac{3.06}{20}\right)} = 2.692\% \text{ per period}$$

or 5.384% per annum.

The true effective rate is 5.40%.

This method produces a rate which is too large on bonds sold at a premium and too small on bonds sold at a discount. The error is due to the fact that the formula is based on arithmetical progression, while the amortized premium or discount increases or decreases periodically in only an approximate arithmetical progression.

DEPRECIATION

Two depreciation methods—the annuity and sinking fund methods—involve compound interest. When the annuity method is used, the investment in the depreciating asset is dealt with as if it were an investment in an annuity. The periodical depreciation charges are analogous to rents and must be large enough to exhaust the cost of the asset, or the cost less residual value, and also provide for the interest. In other words, the charge to operations for depreciation must provide for credits to interest for interest on the gradually diminishing investment, and for credits to the depreciation reserve. The amount of the credit to interest is computed by multiplying the carrying value of the asset (cost less reserve at beginning of period) by the interest rate. The credit to the reserve is the difference between the charge to depreciation and the credit to interest.

When there is no scrap value, the formula for computing the periodical depreciation, is

$$d = \frac{c}{a_{\overline{n}|}}$$

In this formula:

$\quad\quad d$ = periodical depreciation

$\quad\quad c$ = cost of asset

$\quad\quad a_{\overline{n}|}$ = present value of annuity of 1

Illustration: what is the annual depreciation on an asset costing $5,000 which will have no value at the end of five years, if depreciation is to be computed by the annuity method using a rate of 5%? Present value at 5% of 1 due 5 periods hence is .783526166.

Then .216473834 ÷ .05 = 4.32947668, or $a_{\overline{5}|}$

$$d = \frac{5000}{4.32947668} = 1,154.87.$$

The annual depreciation entries may be tabulated thus:

Year	Debit depreciation	Credit interest	Credit reserve	Carrying value
				5,000.00
1	1,154.87	250.00	904.87	4,095.13
2	1,154.87	204.76	950.11	3,145.02
3	1,154.87	157.25	997.62	2,147.40
4	1,154.87	107.37	1,047.50	1,099.90
5	1,154.87	55.00	1,099.87	.03

When there is a scrap value, the formula is:

$$d = \frac{c - (s \times P)}{a_{\overline{n}|}}$$

In which the symbol s represents scrap-value and P represents the present value of 1.

Assuming that the asset in the preceding illustration will have a residual value of $2,000 at the end of 5 years, what should be the annual depreciation?

The present value of 1 at 5% due in 5 periods, was stated·in the illustration to be .783526166; and the present value of an annuity of 1 for 5 periods at 5% was computed above, as 4.32947668. Then

$$d = \frac{5000 - (2000 \times .783526166)}{4.32947668} = 792.92.$$

The annual depreciation entries may be tabulated thus:

Year	Debit depreciation	Credit interest	Credit reserve	Carrying value
				5,000.00
1	792.92	250.00	542.92	4,457.08
2	792.92	222.85	570.07	3,887.01
3	792.92	194.35	598.57	3,288.44
4	792.92	164.42	628.50	2,659.94
5	792.92	133.00	659.92	2,000.02

The sinking fund method is based on the assumption that a fund is created at compound interest to equal the total depreciation. If a fund is created, the contribution is computed in accordance with the formula already stated and explained, namely:

$$S.F.C. = S.F. \div s_{\overline{n}|}$$

Since the total fund required is the difference between the cost and the scrap value of the asset, the formula for determining the periodical contribution to the fund is

$$S.F.C. = \frac{c - s}{s_{\overline{n}|}}$$

Illustration: what annual contribution should be made to a fund on a 5% basis, compounded annually, to provide for an asset costing $5,000 and expected to have a residual value of $2,000 at the expiration of 5 years? And what should be the annual entries for the fund and the depreciation reserve? $1.05^5 = 1.276282$.

$$s_{\overline{5}|} = .276282 \div .05 = 5.52564$$

$$S.F.C. = \frac{5000 - 2000}{5.52564} = 542.92$$

TABLE OF FUND ENTRIES

Year	Debit fund	Credit interest	Credit cash	Balance fund
1	542.92		542.92	542.92
2	570.07	27.15	542.92	1,112.99
3	598.57	55.65	542.92	1,711.56
4	628.50	85.58	542.92	2,340.06
5	659.92	117.00	542.92	2,999.98

The reserve should keep pace with the fund so that at the end of the anticipated life of the asset, the fund and the reserve each will equal the total depreciation. Therefore the amount charged each year to the fund, as shown in the "debit fund" column, should be charged to depreciation and credited to the reserve for depreciation.

SOLUTIONS TO ACTUARIAL PROBLEMS IN THE AMERICAN INSTITUTE EXAMINATIONS

As this book is designed to assist those who expect to be candidates in the examinations set by the American Institute of Accountants, the following problems and solutions are given. These are all the problems in actuarial science given in the Institute examinations at the time of publishing this book.

PROBLEM 1

(JUNE 1917)

A machine costing $81.00 is estimated to have a life of four years, with a residual value of $16.00. Prepare a statement showing the annual charge for depreciation according to each of the following methods:

(a) Straight line.
(b) Constant percentage of diminishing value.
(c) Annuity method.

(For convenience in arithmetical calculation assume the rate of interest to be 10%.)

SOLUTION PROBLEM I

(a) The straight-line method does not require the application of actuarial science, the annual depreciation being computed as follows:

$$\frac{81.00 - 16.00}{4} = 16.25$$

The required statement follows:

Year	Depreciation	Carrying Value
		81.00
1	16.25	64.75
2	16.25	48.50
3	16.25	32.25
4	16.25	16.00
Total	65.00	

(b) The constant percentage of diminishing value method requires the following computation to determine the rate.

$$\text{Rate} = 1 - \sqrt[4]{\frac{16}{81}}$$

Fortunately for the person who is required to solve this problem, both the numerator and denominator of the fraction $\frac{16}{81}$ are fourth powers of integers. 16 is the fourth power of 2, and 81 is the fourth power of 3.

$$\text{Hence} \quad \sqrt[4]{\frac{16}{81}} = \frac{2}{3}$$

$$\text{and } r = 1 - \frac{2}{3}$$
$$= \frac{1}{3}$$

Usually it is necessary to employ logarithms to determine the rate to be applied to the diminishing value. The computation by logarithms is therefore shown although the applicant in an examination could not be expected to submit a logarithmic solution.

$$r = 1 - \sqrt[4]{\frac{16}{81}}$$

Log 16 = 1.204120 or 11.204120 − 10
Log 81 = 1.908485

Then 11.204120 − 10
Minus 1.908485
9.295635 − 10 = Log 16/81

Extract the 4th root:

9.295635 − 10
Add   30   − 30
39.295635 − 40

Divide by 4:

$$\frac{39.295635 - 40}{4} = 9.823909 - 10, \text{ the log of } \sqrt[4]{16/81}$$

9.823909 − 10 is the log of .6666+

Then r = 1 − .6666 = .3333

The required table follows:

Year		Depreciation	Carrying value 81.00
1	(⅓ of 81.00)	27.00	54.00
2	(⅓ of 54.00)	18.00	36.00
3	(⅓ of 36.00)	12.00	24.00
4	(⅓ of 24.00)	8.00	16.00
		65.00	

(c) The annual depreciation according to the annuity method is computed by the formula

$$d = \frac{c - (P \times s)}{D \div i}$$

In this formula

 c = cost   = \$81.00
 s = scrap value   = \$16.00
 P = present value of 1 for 4 periods at 10%
          $1.10^4 = 1.4641$
   $.4641 \div 1.4641 = .31699$ compound discount
and $1 - .31699 = .68301$ present value

Then $d = \dfrac{81 - (.68301 \times 16)}{.31699 \div .10}$

$$= \frac{81 - 10.92816}{3.1699}$$

$$= 22.11$$

The required table follows:

Year	Interest credited	Depreciation debited	Carrying value
			81.00
1	8.10	22.11	66.99
2	6.70	22.11	51.58
3	5.16	22.11	34.63
4	3.46	22.11	15.98
Total	23.42	88.44	

PROBLEM 2

(JUNE 1917)

Argument has been strongly urged that aside from any question of possible mismanagement, or of the difficulty of making satisfactory investments to yield the same rate as is paid on the bonds, a sinking fund for bonds is more expensive than an arrangement for the serial repayment of bonds. This is illustrated by the case of $20,000 5% bonds. If these are paid off in a series, one each year, the total payment made will be principal $20,000, interest $10,500, total $30,500. The annual sinking fund to pay these bonds would on a 5% basis amount to $604.85, making in twenty years $12,097, and the interest paid on the bonds would be $20,000, total payments $32,097. The apparent excess burden is accordingly $1,597.

Discuss the above argument and show clearly just what the figures mean and in what the apparent saving actually consists.

Solution Problem 2

The disadvantage of the sinking fund plan is apparent only, and not real. The apparent excess burden of $1,597 is due to the fact that during the early years more principal is provided for under the serial redemption plan than under the sinking fund plan. Since the borrower has more use of the money under the sinking fund plan than under the serial redemption plan, the necessity of paying more interest under this plan cannot be said to be a disadvantage.

The relative advantages of these two plans may be made more apparent by a brief discussion of a third plan, known as the annuity method. By this method equal annual payments would be made, these payments including the interest accrued to date and a payment on the principal. The annual payments under the annuity plan would be computed as follows:

The $20,000 principal is the present value of the 20 payments or rents of unknown amount which will pay the principal sum and the interest.

.376889 is the present value of 1 at 5% due 20 periods hence
.623111 is the compound discount
.613111 ÷ .05 = 12.4622 the present value of an annuity of 1 for 20 periods
20,000 ÷ 12.4622 = 1604.85 the equal annual payment to be made under the annuity plan.

At the end of the first year there will be $1,000.00 accrued interest; the remaining $604.85 will apply on the principal. The operation of the three plans during the first year may be compared thus:

	Serial redemption	Sinking fund	Annuity redemption
Interest	1,000.00	1,000.00	1,000.00
Payment on principal	1,000.00	604.85	604.85
Remaining principal	19,000.00	19,395.15	19,395.15

Since the principal unprovided for during the second year is greater under the sinking fund and the annuity plans than under the serial plan, it is reasonable to expect the interest expense of the second year to be larger under these plans. The interest on these excesses during the entire life of the loan exactly accounts. for the $1,597.00, as shown by the following comparative table:

SERIAL REDEMPTION PLAN

Year	Total disbursement	Payment of interest	Payment on principal	Balance of principal
				20,000.00
1	2,000.00	1,000.00	1,000.00	19,000.00
2	1,950.00	950.00	1,000.00	18,000.00
3	1,900.00	900.00	1,000.00	17,000.00
4	1,850.00	850.00	1,000.00	16,000.00
5	1,800.00	800.00	1,000.00	15,000.00
6	1,750.00	750.00	1,000.00	14,000.00
7	1,700.00	700.00	1,000.00	13,000.00
8	1,650.00	650.00	1,000.00	12,000.00
9	1,600.00	600.00	1,000.00	11,000.00
10	1,550.00	550.00	1,000.00	10,000.00
11	1,500.00	500.00	1,000.00	9,000.00
12	1,450.00	450.00	1,000.00	8,000.00
13	1,400.00	400.00	1,000.00	7,000.00
14	1,350.00	350.00	1,000.00	6,000.00
15	1,300.00	300.00	1,000.00	5,000.00
16	1,250.00	250.00	1,000.00	4,000.00
17	1,200.00	200.00	1,000.00	3,000.00
18	1,150.00	150.00	1,000.00	2,000.00
19	1,100.00	100.00	1,000.00	1,000.00
20	1,050.00	50.00	1,000.00	0.00 [1]
	30,500.00	10,500.00	20,000.00	

Sinking Fund and Annuity Plans

Year	Total disbursement	Payment of interest	Payment on principal	Balance of principal
				20,000.00
1	1,604.85	,000.00	604.85	19,395.15
2	1,604.85	969.76	635.09	18,760.06
3	1,604.85	938.00	666.85	18,093.21
4	1,604.85	904.66	700.19	17,393.02
5	1,604.85	869.65	735.20	16,657.82
6	1,604.85	832.89	771.96	15,885.86
7	1,604.85	794.29	810.56	15,075.30
8	1,604.85	753.77	851.08	14,224.22
9	1,604.85	711.21	893.64	13,330.58
10	1,604.85	666.53	938.32	12,392.26
11	1,604.85	619.61	985.24	11,407.02
12	1,604.85	570.35	1,034.50	10,372.52
13	1,604.85	518.63	1,086.22	9,286.30
14	1,604.85	464.32	1,140.53	8,145.77
15	1,604.85	407.29	1,197.56	6,948.21
16	1,604.85	347.41	1,257.44	5,690.77
17	1,604.85	284.54	1,320.31	4,370.46
18	1,604.85	218.52	1,386.33	2,984.13
19	1,604.85	149.21	1,455.64	1,528.49
20	1,604.85	76.42	1,528.43	.06
	32,097.00	12,097.06	19,999.94	

By comparing the two "Balance of Principal" columns it will be seen that after the first year, the principal is always larger under the sinking fund and annuity plans than under the serial redemption plan. Therefore the interest under the sinking fund plan is larger than under the serial plan. But so long as the interest is proportionate to the principal, this cannot be said to be a disadvantage.

PROBLEM 3

(NOVEMBER 1917)

You are called upon to state what is the annual sinking fund necessary to redeem a principal sum of $1,000,000 due 30 years hence—it being assumed that the annual sums set aside are invested at compound interest at 5 per cent. State what computations you would make to arrive at the result desired. You need not work out the computation.

SOLUTION PROBLEM 3

Assuming that the contributions are deposited at the end of each year, the annual sum would be computed by dividing the required fund of $1,000,000 by the amount of an ordinary annuity of $1 for 30 periods at 5%.

The amount of an ordinary annuity of $1.00 for 30 periods at 5% would be computed by dividing the compound interest on $1.00 for 30 periods at 5% by the simple interest rate 5%.

The compound interest would be computed by raising 1.05 to the 30th power, and deducting 1 therefrom.

Or, stated in the order of procedure, the annual contribution would be computed thus:

Raise 1.05 to the 30th power, thus:

$$1.05 \times 1.05 = 1.05^2$$
$$1.05^2 \times 1.05^2 = 1.05^4$$
$$1.05^4 \times 1.05^4 = 1.05^8$$
$$1.05^8 \times 1.05^8 = 1.05^{16}$$
$$1.05^{16} \times 1.05^8 = 1.05^{24}$$
$$1.05^{24} \times 1.05^4 = 1.05^{28}$$
$$1.05^{28} \times 1.05^2 = 1.05^{30}$$

Compute the compound interest, I, which is $1.05^{30} - 1$

Divide the value of I by .05 to compute the amount of an annuity of 1, represented by $s_{\overline{n}|}$.

Divide \$1,000,000 by $s_{\overline{n}|}$ to determine the annual contribution.

PROBLEM 4

(NOVEMBER 1917)

A owns an annuity of \$50 per annum, the first payment on which falls due one year hence, and which continues for a period of twenty years certain. State:

(a) The present value of the benefit
(b) The amount which he will have accumulated at the end of the period if he invests each moiety as it becomes due.

Assume interest at 4 per cent payable annually. In this connection the value of $(1.04)^{20}$ is stated to be equal to 2.191123.

SOLUTION PROBLEM 4

(a) The present value of the benefit or annuity
is computed by dividing the compound
discount by the simple interest rate of 4%.
Since the compound discount is not stated
in the problem it must be computed. Since
the problem states the amount of 1 at 4%
for 20 periods the easiest way to compute
the compound discount is to divide the
compound interest on 1 by the amount of 1.

2.191123 = amount of 1 for 20 periods at 4%
1.000000

1.191123 = compound interest on 1 for 20 periods at 4%

And 1.191123 ÷ 2.191123 = .543613, compound discount
Then .543613 ÷ .04 = 13.590325, present value of annuity of 1
And 13.590325 × 50 = 679.52, present value of annuity of 50

(b) The amount which will have accumulated at
the end of the period if each moiety or rent
is invested as it becomes due, is the amount
of an ordinary annuity of $50.00 per
period for 20 periods invested at 4%. The
amount of an annuity of $1 is computed
by dividing the compound interest on 1 at
4% for 20 periods by the simple interest
rate of 4%; the amount of an annuity of
1 should then be multiplied by 50.

2.191123   amount of 1 at 4% for 20 periods
1.000000
_____
1.191123   compound interest on 1 at 4% for 20 periods.

1.191123÷.04=29.778075, amount of annuity of 1
29.778075× 50=1488.90   "   "   "   "   50

PROOF OF PRESENT VALUE OF $679.52

Period	Rent	Interest	Reduction	Balance
				679.52
1	50.00	27.18	22.82	656.70
2	50.00	26.27	23.73	632.97
3	50.00	25.32	24.68	608.29
4	50.00	24.33	25.67	582.62
5	50.00	23.30	26.70	555.92
6	50.00	22.24	27.76	528.16
7	50.00	21.13	28.87	499.29
8	50.00	19.97	30.03	469.26
9	50.00	18.77	31.23	438.03
10	50.00	17.52	32.48	405.55
11	50.00	16.22	33.78	371.77
12	50.00	14.87	35.13	336.64
13	50.00	13.47	36.53	300.11
14	50.00	12.00	38.00	262.11
15	50.00	10.48	39.52	222.59
16	50.00	8.90	41.10	181.49
17	50.00	7.26	42.74	138.75
18	50.00	5.55	44.45	94.30
19	50.00	3.78	46.22	48.08
20	50.00	1.92	48.08	.00
Totals	1,000.00	320.48	679.52	

PROOF OF AMOUNT OF $1,488.90

Period	Interest	Rent	Amount
1		50.00	50.00
2	2.00	50.00	102.00
3	4.08	50.00	156.08
4	6.24	50.00	212.32
5	8.49	50.00	270.81
6	10.83	50.00	331.64
7	13.27	50.00	394.91
8	15.80	50.00	460.71
9	18.43	50.00	529.14
10	21.17	50.00	600.31
11	24.01	50.00	674.32
12	26.97	50.00	751.29
13	30.05	50.00	831.34
14	33.25	50.00	914.59
15	36.58	50.00	1,001.17
16	40.05	50.00	1,091.22
17	43.65	50.00	1,184.87
18	47.40	50.00	1,282.27
19	51.29	50.00	1,383.56
20	55.34	50.00	1,488.90
Totals	488.90	1000.00	

PROBLEM 5

(MAY 1918)

In auditing the books of a corporation you find that, in order to provide a sum to redeem a mortgage of $100,000.00 falling due at the end of 10 years, a reserve of $8,000.00 per annum has been set aside annually for three years, but that, contrary to intention, the company has failed to accumulate interest thereon. Assuming interest at 4 per cent. (convertible annually) what should have been the total accumulations to date, and what amount should now be set aside annually for the next seven years in order to complete the sinking fund? $(1.04)^7 = 1.31593$.

SOLUTION PROBLEM 5

This problem may be construed in several ways. The first uncertainty of meaning is caused by using the word "reserve." A reserve is an account with a credit balance set up, usually, by a charge to profit and loss or to surplus.

Under a strict definition of the word "reserve," the problem means that an entry has been made for the appropriation of surplus by charging surplus and crediting a reserve, and that no fund has been set aside, since none is mentioned. The examiners, however, may have used the word "reserve" to convey the idea that a fund has been set aside. We have two possible conditions, therefore:

(a)   A reserve of $24,000, but no fund
(b)   A fund of $24,000.

The following question is also uncertain in meaning: "Assuming interest at 4 per cent (convertible annually) what should have been the total accumulation to date?" Do the examiners want to know

1. How much the three $8,000 deposits would have amounted to. if invested at 4%? If so, the solution is:

$1.04^3 = 1.124864$ amount of 1 at 4% for 3 periods
$.124864 \div .04 = 3.1216$ amount of annuity of 1 at 4% for 3 periods
$3.1216 \times 8,000. = 24,972.80$ amount which would be on hand.

2. Or, do they wish to know how much should have been on hand if the corporation had computed the annual contributions to the fund on a strict actuarial basis, and had accumulated interest thereon? If so, the solution is:

$1.04^7 = 1.31593$ (per problem)
$1.04^3 = 1.124864$ (as above)
$1.04^{10} = 1.04^7 \times 1.04^3 = 1.31593 \times 1.124864 = 1.480242$
$.480242 \div .04 = 12.00605$ amount of annuity of 1 for 10 periods at 4%
$100,000 \div 12.00605 = 8,329.13$ annual contribution
Amount of annuity of 1 for 3 periods, as above $= 3.1216$
$8,329.13 \times 3.1216 = 26,000.21$ amount which would be on hand.

The second part of the question is: "What amount should now be set aside annually for the next seven years in order to complete the sinking fund?"

(a) If there is a reserve of $24,000 but no fund at the date of the audit, the entire $100,000 will have to be provided by the seven contributions and interest thereon.

$1.04^7 = 1.31593$

$.31593 \div .04 = 7.89825$ amount of annuity of 1 at 4% for 7 periods

$100,000 \div 7.89825 = 12,661.03$ periodical contribution

(b) If there is already a fund of $24,000 this fund will draw interest for the remainder of the 10 years. Since the first three contributions would normally have been made at the end of the first three years, the remaining seven payments would begin at the end of the fourth year. This would mean that although seven more deposits are to be made there are only six years until the maturity of the mortgage.

$1.31593 \div 1.04 = 1.26532$, value of 1.04^6

$1.26532 \times 24,000 = 30,367.68$ amount to which 24,000 will accumulate.

Total fund required	100,000.00
24,000.00 and interest thereon	30,367.68
Balance to be provided by 7 installments	69,632.32

$69,632.32 \div 7.89825 = 8,816.18$ annual contribution.

PROBLEM 6

(NOVEMBER 1918)

A corporation wants to retire a debt of $105,000 bearing 5% interest payable annually. The tenth payment, including interest, is to be $15,000. The other nine periodical payments are all to include interest and to be of the same amount. Required the amount of each of such nine payments. $(1.05^9 = 1.551328.)$

SOLUTION PROBLEM 6

The words "retire a debt" indicate that the payments are to be made to the creditor and not into a sinking fund. Since the last payment of $15,000 covers the balance of the principal unpaid at the beginning of the tenth year with 5% interest thereon, this $15,000 payment must be 1.05 times the balance unpaid at the beginning of the tenth year.

Hence, $15,000.00 ÷ 1.05 = $14,285.71 balance unpaid at beginning of 10th year.

$105,000.00 total debt.

   14,285.71 principal liquidated by 10th payment]

$90,714.29   "   "   " first 9 payments

Then $90,714.29 is the present value at 5% of nine unknown annual payments, which are computed thus:

Then .551328 (comp. int.)÷1.551328 (amt. of 1)=.355391 compound discount on 1 for 9 periods at 5%

.355391÷.05=7.10782 present value of annuity of 1 for 9
periods at 5%, or principal which would be paid by 9
annual installments of $1.00

90,714.29÷7.10782=12,762.60 number of dollars in each of
the first 9 annual payments made in liquidation of
$90,714.29 of principal, and interest thereon.

In addition to the annual payments of $12,-762.60 which liquidate $90,714.29 and the interest on the diminishing balance thereof during the first nine years, the corporation must pay during each of these years 5% interest on the $14,285.71 unpaid at the beginning of the tenth year. 5% of $14,285.71 is $714.29.

SUMMARY

$12,762.60	annual payment during first 9 years on $90,714.29
714.29	annual interest " " " " " 14,285.71
$13,476.89	total

PROOF
Annual Payment

Year	Total	Interest	Principal	Balance
				105,000.00
1	13,476.89	5,250.00	8,226.89	96,773.11
2	13,476.89	4,838.66	8,638.23	88,134.88
3	13,476.89	4,406.74	9,070.15	79,064.73
4	13,476.89	3,953.24	9,523.65	69,541.08
5	13,476.89	3,477.05	9,999.84	59,541.24
6	13,476.89	2,977.06	10,499.83	49,041.41
7	13,476.89	2,452.07	11,024.82	38,016.59
8	13,476.89	1,900.83	11,576.06	26,440.53
9	13,476.89	1,322.03	12,154.86	14,285.67
10	15,000.00	714.28	14,285.72	
Totals	136,292.01	31,291.96	105,000.05	

There is an over payment of five cents, a dis-crepancy too small to be avoided.

PROBLEM 7
(NOVEMBER 1918)

A $10,000 five per cent semi-annual coupon bond is bought on a 4 per cent basis, due 1½ years hence. What did it cost?

SOLUTION PROBLEM 7

Since the bond is due in 1½ years and bears semi-annual coupons, there are 3 interest periods and the effective rate is 2% per period. The cost of the bond may be computed in two different ways, but in either case the present value of an annuity of 1 at 2% for 3 periods will be required, and it is therefore computed thus:

1.000000 ÷ 1.02 = .980392 P.V. of 1 at 2% due 1 period hence
.980392 ÷ 1.02 = .961169 "   "   1 " 2%   " 2 periods   "
.961169 ÷ 1.02 = .942322 "   "   1 " 2%   " 3   "   "
1 − .942322 = .057678 compound discount
.057678 ÷ .02 = 2.8839 P. V. of annuity of 1 at 2% for 3 periods

First Method:

Find the present value of all benefits under the bond, discounted at 2%:

Par (10,000.00)
    .942322 (P. V. of 1 due 3 periods hence) × 10,000 =   9,423.22
Coupons (250.00 each)
    2.8839 (P. V. of annuity of 1 for 3 periods) × 250 =   720.98
                                  10,144.20

Second Method:

Find the present value discounted at the effective interest rate, of an annuity whose rents are equal to the difference between the interest at the nominal rate and at the effective rate on par. The present value of this annuity is the premium.

$2\frac{1}{2}\%$ of $10,000 = \$250.00$ nominal interest on par
2% " $10,000 = 200.00$ effective " " "
_____
50.00 difference

50.00×2.8839 (P. V. of Annuity) $= 144.195$ premium
$10,000.00$ par
144.20 premium
_____
$10,144.20$ cost of bond.

PROOF

Period	Coupon	Effective interest	Premium amortized	Carrying value
				10,144.20
1	250.00	202.88	47.12	10,097.08
2	250.00	201.94	48.06	10,049.02
3	250.00	200.98	49.02	10,000.00
	750.00	605.80	144.20	

PROBLEM 8

(MAY 1919)

A bond, bearing interest at 5% per annum payable annually, and repayable in five years, with bonus of 10%, is for sale. What price can a purchaser pay who desires to realize 6% on his investment? $(V^5$ at $6\% = .7473)$

SOLUTION PROBLEM 8

When a bond is repayable at a premium, the best method of computing the price is to find the present value of the benefits to be received, thus:

Par plus 10% bonus:
> Assuming a par of $1,000.00 the payment at
> maturity would be $1,100.00
> Then 1,100×.7473 (P.V. of 1 in 5 periods at 6%)= 822.03

Coupons:
> 1−.7473=.2527   compound discount
> .2527÷.06=4.2116 P. V. of annuity of 1
> 50.00 (Coupons)×4.2116=   210.58
> Total price   1,032.61

PROOF

Year	Coupon	Effective income	Amortization	Carrying value
				1,032.61
1	50.00	61.96	11.96	1,044.57
2	50.00	62.67	12.67	1,057.24
3	50.00	63.43	13.43	1,070.67
4	50.00	64.24	14.24	1,084.91
5	50.00	65.09	15.09	1,100.00
	250.00	317.39	67.39	

PROBLEM 9
(MAY 1919)

A lease has five years to run at $1,000.00 a year payable at the end of each year, with an extension for a further five years at $1,200.00 a year. On a 6% basis what sum should be paid now in lieu of the ten years' rent? (V^5 at 6% = ·7473)

SOLUTION PROBLEM 9

The sum to be paid for the first 5 rents of $1,000.00 each is the present value of an ordinary annuity, computed as follows:

·7473 present value of 1 at 6% for 5 periods

1−·7473=·2527 compound discount

·2527÷·06=4.211667 P. V. of ordinary annuity of 1 at 6% for 5 periods

4.211667×1,000=4,211.67 P. V. of ordinary annuity of 1000 at 6% for 5 periods or amount to be paid as present value of first 5 rents.

The sum to be paid for the last 5 rents of $1,200.00 each is the present value of an annuity of 5 rents at 6%, deferred 5 periods. An ordinary annuity of 5 rents of $1,200.00 is computed thus:

4.211667 ×1200=5,054.00   P.V. of ordinary annuity.

Then 5,054.00×·7473=3,776.85   P.V. of annuity deferred 5 periods

SUMMARY

$4,211.67   present value of first 5 rents of $1,000.00 each

3,776.85   "   "   " last 5 rents of $1,200.00   "

$7,988.52   total to be paid.

PROOF

The $7,988.52 would be charged to leasehold premium, and at the close of each year, journal entries would be made

Debiting Rent ($1,000 first five years, $1,200 last five)

Crediting Interest (6% of balance of lease-hold premium account)

Crediting Leasehold Premium (enough to balance the journal entry)

If $7,988.52 is the correct present value, the entry at the end of the fifth year should reduce the leasehold account to $5,054.00, the present value as shown above of an ordinary annuity at 6% of five rents of $1,200 each, and the entry at the end of the tenth year should close the account.

TABLE OF ENTRIES

End of year	Debit rent	Credit interest	Credit leasehold premium	Balance leasehold premium
				7,988.52
1	1,000.00	479.31	520.69	7,467.83
2	1,000.00	448.07	551.93	6,915.90
3	1,000.00	414.95	585.05	6,330.85
4	1,000.00	379.85	620.15	5,710.70
5	1,000.00	342.64	657.36	5,053.34

At this point a discrepancy appears. The balance should be $5,054.00 and it is $5,053.34 instead. The present value, .7453 is not sufficiently exact for the purposes of this problem; therefore the value of V^5 @ 6% will be computed and the problem resolved:

$$1 \div 1.06 = .943396226$$
$$.943396226 \div 1.06 = .889996440$$
$$.889996440 \div 1.06 = .839619283$$
$$.839619283 \div 1.06 = .792093663$$
$$.792093663 \div 1.06 = .747258173$$ P.V. of 1 at 6% due 5 periods hence

$$1 - .747258173 = .252741827$$ compound discount

$$.252741827 \div .06 = 4.2123637$$ P.V. of ordinary annuity of 1 at 6% for 5 periods

$$4.2123637 \times 1000 = 4,212.3637$$ P.V. of ordinary annuity of 1000 at 6% for 5 periods, or amount to be paid as present value of first 5 rents

$$4.2123637 \times 1200 = 5,054.83644$$ P.V. of ordinary annuity of 1200 at 6% for 5 periods

$$5,054.83644 \times .747258173 = 3,777.2678$$ P. V. of deferred annuity

SUMMARY

$4,212.3637	P.V. of first 5 rents; $1,000 each
3,777.2678	" of last 5 rents; 1,200 "
$7,989.6315	total

PROOF

End of year	Debit rent	Credit interest	Credit leasehold premium	Balance leasehold premium
				7,989.63
1	1,000.00	479.38	520.62	7,469.01
2	1,000.00	448.14	551.86	6,917.15
3	1,000.00	415.03	584.97	6,332.18
4	1,000.00	379.93	620.07	5,712.11
5	1,000.00	342.73	657.27	5,054.84
6	1,200.00	303.29	896.71	4,158.13
7	1,200.00	249.49	950.51	3,207.62
8	1,200.00	192.46	1,007.54	2,200.08
9	1,200.00	132.00	1,068.00	1,132.08
10	1,200.00	67.92	1,132.08	0
	11,000.00	3,010.37	7,989.63	

Problem 10
(May 1920)

The maximum sum insured under the soldiers' insurance with the government is payable $57.50 per month for 20 years certain after death or disability. How can the equivalent sum payable in cash be found? Give the correct formula and explain why 12 x 57.50 x $A_{\overline{20|}}$ differs from the equivalent cash sum.

Given: A_{20} at $3\frac{1}{2} = 14.21$

Solution 10

The problem is indefinite as to whether the first monthly payment is due immediately after death or disability, or one month thereafter. This is immaterial, however, if it is assumed that "the equivalent sum payable in cash" is payable on the same date that the first monthly payment would have been made.

If the monthly payments were made they would constitute an annuity due of 240 rents of $57.50 each, payable monthly. The formula 12 x 57.50 x $a_{\overline{20|}}$ is not correct for two reasons.

In the first place, $14.21, the value of $a_{\overline{20|}}$ at $3\frac{1}{2}\%$, is the present value of an *ordinary* annuity, while the annuity in question is an annuity *due*. That is, $14.21 is the present value of an annuity the rents of which are payable at the end of each period, while in this case the rents are payable at the beginning of each period, since it is assumed that the equivalent cash sum is payable on the date when the first monthly installment would have been due.

In the second place, the formula 12 x 57.50 x $a_{\overline{20|}}$ is based on the assumption that twenty annual payments are to be made, each of which is 12 x 57.50, or $690. The facts are that 240 monthly payments are to be made of $57.50 each. The annual rate is therefore only nominal; the effective rate is 3½% divided by 12, or 7–24%.

Therefore, instead of using $a_{\overline{20|}}$ at 3½%, or 14.21, it will be necessary to use the present value of an annuity due of 240 rents at 7–24%. The present value of an annuity due of 240 rents is computed by finding the present value of an ordinary annuity of 239 rents and adding 1 rent. This could be represented by $a_{\overline{239|}}$ +1, the rate being 7–24%. The formula would be 57.50 x ($a_{\overline{239|}}$ +1).

Problem 11
(May 1920)

The 4¾% Victory notes mature at par on May 20, 1923. If a purchaser buys at $96.20 on May 20, 1920, calculate the approximate yield per cent.

Given:	2¾%	3%
A_6=	5.4624	5.4172
V^6=	.8498	.8375

Solution 11

The approximate rate can be computed by determining what the price would have been if the bond had been purchased at an effective rate of 2¾% per period of six months; also what the price would have been on a basis of 3% per period. The difference between these prices caused by an increase of ¼% in the rate will serve as an approximate measure of the excess of the effective rate over 2¾% when the purchase was made at $96.20.

Price on a basis of 2¾% per six months:

Effective rate on par	2.75
Nominal " " "	2.375
Difference	.375
Multiply by Pres. Val. of annuity at 2¾%	5.4624
Discount	2.0484
Par	100.00
Discount	2.05
Price	97.95

Price on a basis of 3% per six months:

Effective rate on par	3.00
Nominal " " "	2.375
Difference	.625
Multiply by Pres. Val. of annuity at 3%	5.4172
Discount	3.38575
Par	100.00
Discount	3.39
Price	96.61

At an effective rate of 2¾% the price would be   97.95
"   "   "   "   " 3 % "   "   "   "   96.61

An increase of   ¼% reduces the price   1.34

Price on basis of 2¾% per period   97.95
"   " unknown basis   96.20

Decrease in price   1.75

Now if a decrease of $1.34 in the price is caused by an increase of ¼% in the rate, the decrease of $1.75 in the price is caused by an increase of approximately $\frac{1.75}{1.34}$ of ¼% or .3265%.

Then 2.75% plus .3265% = 3.0765%, the approximate rate per period, and 6.153% is the approximate rate per annum.

SCHEDULE OF AMORTIZATION

Date	Coupon	Effective Income	Discount Amortized	Value
May 20, 1920				96.20
Nov. 20, 1920	2.38	2.96	.58	96.78
May 20, 1921	2.37	2.98	.61	97.39
Nov. 20, 1921	2.38	3.00	.62	98.01
May 20, 1922	2.37	3.02	.65	98.66
Nov. 20, 1922	2.38	3.04	.66	99.32
May 20, 1923	2.37	3.06	.69	100.01
	14.25	18.06	3.81	

This schedule shows that the 3.0765% rate is an unusually close approximation.

Problem 12

(May 1920)

A company is issuing $100,000 of 4% 20-year bonds, which it wishes to pay at maturity by means of a sinking fund, in which equal annual deposits are to be made. The board of directors wishes to assume that this fund will earn $5\frac{1}{2}\%$ interest for the first five years, 5% for the next five years and 4% for the last ten years. What is the annual deposit required?

Given:	$5\frac{1}{2}\%$	5%	4%
S_5	5.581	5.526	5.416
S_{10}	12.875	12.578	12.006
$(1+i)^5$	1.307	1.276	1.217
$(1+i)^{10}$	1.708	1.629	1.480

Solution 12

The problem states that the directors wish "to assume that this fund will earn $5\frac{1}{2}\%$ interest for the first five years, 5% for the next five years and 4% for the last ten years." It is doubtful whether the examiners intended this statement to be interpreted literally. The fund will not earn $5\frac{1}{2}\%$ interest during the first five years unless the first despoit is made at the beginning of the first year. This is not customary and besides it would require a recom-

putation of the various present values stated
in the problem, converting them from present
values of ordinary annuities to present values of
annuities due.

The problem will be solved first on the
assumption that the deposits are made at the
end of each year, in which case the fund will
earn 5½% interest during the second, third,
fourth and fifth years, 5% during the next five
years, and 4% during the last ten years. It will
then be solved on the basis of a literal inter-
pretation of the statement of prospective interest
earnings.

It is regrettable that the values stated in the
problem are not carried to six decimal places;
the three place numbers are not exact enough to
permit proving the correctness of the sinking
fund contribution. In the solutions which fol-
low, the first column shows the results obtained
by using the three place values stated in the
problem; the second column shows the results
obtained by using six place values.

Computation on assumption that contributions to the fund are made at the end of each
year:

First five contributions: (3 place)   (6 place)

	(3 place)	(6 place)
Amount at end of first five years	5.581	5.581091
Multiply by $(1.05)^5$	1.276	1.276281
Amt. of 1st five contributions at end of 10th year	7.121356	7.123040
Multiply by $(1.04)^{10}$	1.480	1.480244
Amount of 1st five contributions at end of 20th year	10.539607	10.543837

Next five contributions:

Amount at end of tenth year	5.526	5.525631
Multiply by $(1.04)^{10}$	1.480	1.480244
Amount of 2nd five contributions at end 20 year	8.17848	8.179282

Next ten contributions:

Amount at end of 20th year	12.006	12.006107

Summary:

First five contributions amount to	10.539607	10.543837
Next five " " "	8.17848	8.179282
Next ten " " "	12.006	12.006107
Total	30.724087	30.729226

Sinking Fund Contribution:

100,000 divided by 30.724,087 =	3,254.78	
100,000 " " 30.729,226 =		3,254.23

The following schedule of accumulation is prepared by way of proof, although the applicant is not required and would probably not have time to prepare it in the examination.

ACCUMULATION OF FUND

First	Year	Contribution	3,254.78	3,254.23
Second	"	Interest at 5½%	179.01	178.98
		Contribution	3,254.78	3,254.23
		Total	6,688.57	6,687.44
Third	"	Interest at 5½%	367.87	367.81
		Contribution	3,254.78	3,254.23
		Total	10,311.22	10,309.48
Fourth	"	Interest at 5½%	567.12	567.02
		Contribution	3,254.78	3,254.23
		Total	14,133.12	14,130.73
Fifth	"	Interest at 5½%	777.32	777.19
		Contribution	3,254.78	3,254.23
		Total	18,165.22	18,162.15
Sixth	"	Interest at 5%	908.26	908.11
		Contribution	3,254.78	3,254.23
		Total	22,328.26	22,324.49
Seventh	"	Interest at 5%	1,116.41	1,116.22
		Contribution	3,254.78	3,254.23
		Total	26,699.45	26,694.94
Eighth	"	Interest at 5%	1,334.97	1,334.75
		Contribution	3,254.78	3,254.23
		Total	31,289.20	31,283.92
Ninth	"	Interest at 5%	1,564.46	1,564.20
		Contribution	3,254.78	3,254.23
		Total	36,108.44	36,102.35
Tenth	"	Interest at 5%	1,805.42	1,805.12
		Contribution	3,254.78	3,254.23
		Total	41,168.64	41,161.70

Eleventh Year	Interest at 4%	1,646.75	1,646.47
	Contribution	3,254.78	3,254.23
	Total	46,070.17	46,062.40
Twelfth "	Interest at 4%	1,842.81	1,842.50
	Contribution	3,254.78	3,254.23
	Total	51,167.76	51,159.13
Thirteenth "	Interest at 4%	2,046.71	2,046.37
	Contribution	3,254.78	3,254.23
	Total	56,469.25	56,459.73
Fourteenth "	Interest at 4%	2,258.77	2,258.39
	Contribution	3,254.78	3,254.23
	Total	61,982.80	61,972.35
Fifteenth "	Interest at 4%	2,479.31	2,478.89
	Contribution	3,254.78	3,254.23
	Total	67,716.89	67,705.47
Sixteenth "	Interest at 4%	2,708.68	2,708.22
	Contribution	3,254.78	3,254.23
	Total	73,680.35	73,667.92
Seventeenth "	Interest at 4%	2,947.21	2,946.72
	Contribution	3,254.78	3,254.23
	Total	79,882.34	79,868.87
Eighteenth "	Interest at 4%	3,195.29	3,194.75
	Contribution	3,254.78	3,254.23
	Total	86,332.41	86,317.85
Nineteenth "	Interest at 4%	3,453.30	3,452.71
	Contribution	3,254.78	3,254.23
	Total	93,040.49	93,024.79
Twentieth "	Interest at 4%	3,721.62	3,720.99
	Contribution	3,254.78	3,254.23
	Total	100,016.89	100,000.01

Computation on assumption that contributions are made at the beginning of each year:

First five contributions: (3 place) (6 place)

	(3 place)	(6 place)
Amount of ordinary annuity of 1 for 5 periods at $5\frac{1}{2}\%$	5.581	5.581091
Multiply by	1.055	1.055
Amount of annuity due of 1 for 5 periods at $5\frac{1}{2}\%$	5.887955	5.888051
Multiply by 1.05^5	1.276	1.276281
Amount of first 5 contributions at end of 10th year	7.513030	7.514806
Multiply by 1.04^{10}	1.48	1.480244
Amount of first 5 contributions at end of 20th year	11.119284	11.123750

Next five contributions:

Amount of ordinary annuity of 1 for 5 periods at 5%	5.526	5.525631
Multiply by	1.05	1.05
Amount of annuity due of 1 for 5 periods at 5%	5.8023	5.801913
Multiply by 1.04^{10}	1.48	1.480244
Amount of second 5 contributions at end of 20th year	8.587404	8.588247

Next ten contributions: (3 place) (6 place)

	(3 place)	(6 place)
Amount of ordinary annuity of 1 for 10 periods at 4%	12.006	12.006107
Multiply by	1.04	1.04
Amount of annuity due of 1 for 10 periods at 4%	12.48624	12.486351

Summary:

First five contributions amount to	11.119284	11.123750
Next five " " "	8.587404	8.588247
Next ten " " "	12.48624	12.486351
Total	32.192928	32.198348

Sinking Fund Contribution:

100,000 divided by 32.192,928=	3,106.27	
100,000 " " 32.198,348=		3,105.75

1st Year	Contribution	3,106.27	3,105.75
	Interest at 5½%	170.84	170.82
2nd "	Contribution	3,106.27	3,105.75
	Total at interest 2nd year	6,383.38	6,382.32
	Interest at 5½%	351.09	351.03
3rd "	Contribution	3,106.27	3,105.75
	Total at interest 3rd year	9,840.74	9,839.10
	Interest at 5½%	541.24	541.15
4th "	Contribution	3,106.27	3,105.75
	Total at interest 4th year	13,488.25	13,486.00
	Interest at 5½%	741.85	741.73
5th "	Contribution	3,106.27	3,105.75
	Total at interest 5th year	17,336.37	17,333.48
	Interest at 5½%	953.50	953.34
6th "	Contribution	3,106.27	3,105.75
	Total at interest 6th year	21,396.14	21,392.57
	Interest at 5%	1,069.81	1,069.63
7th "	Contribution	3,106.27	3,105.75
	Total at interest 7th year	25,572.22	25,567.95
	Interest at 5%	1,278.61	1,278.40

8th Year	Contribution	3,106.27	3,105.75
	Total at interest 8th year	29,957.10	29,952.10
	Interest at 5%	1,497.86	1,497.61
9th "	Contribution	3,106.27	3,105.75
	Total at interest 9th year	34,561.23	34,555.46
	Interest at 5%	1,728.06	1,727.77
10th "	Contribution	3,106.27	3,105.75
	Total at interest 10th year	39,395.56	39,388.98
	Interest at 5%	1,969.78	1,969.45
11th "	Contribution	3,106.27	3,105.75
"	Total at interest 11th year	44,471.61	44,464.18
	Interest at 4%	1,778.86	1,778.57
12th "	Contribution	3,106.27	3,105.75
	Total at interest 12th year	49,356.74	49,348.50
	Interest at 4%	1,974.27	1,973.94
13th "	Contribution	3,106.27	3,105.75
	Total at interest 13th year	54,437.28	54,428.19
	Interest at 4%	2,177.49	2,177.13
14th "	Contribution	3,106.27	3,105.75
	Total at interest 14th year	59,721.04	59,711.07
	Interest at 4%	2,388.84	2,388.44
15th "	Contribution	3,106.27	3,105.75
	Total at interest 15th year	65,216.15	65,205.26
	Interest at 4%	2,608.65	2,608.21
16th "	Contribution	3,106.27	3,105.75
	Total at interest 16th year	70,931.07	70,919.22
	Interest at 4%	2,837.24	2,836.77
17th "	Contribution	3,106.27	3,105.75
	Total at interest 17th year	76,874.58	76,861.74
	Interest at 4%	3,074.98	3,074.47

18th Year	Contribution		3,106.27	3,105.75
	Total at interest 18th year		83,055.83	83,041.96
	Interest at 4%		3,322.23	3,321.68
19th "	Contribution		3,106.27	3,105.75
	Total at interest 19th year		89,484.33	89,469.39
	Interest at 4%		3,579.37	3,578.78
20th "	Contribution		3,106.27	3,105.75
	Total at interest 20th year		96,169.97	96,153.92
	Interest at 4%		3,846.80	3,846.16
	Total		100,016.77	100,000.08

Lightning Source UK Ltd.
Milton Keynes UK
UKHW02f0655060118
315628UK00005B/364/P